Y0-BXI-938

Remembering Made Easy

Jacqueline Dineen

© COPYRIGHT 1979 AND PUBLISHED BY
COLES PUBLISHING COMPANY LIMITED
TORONTO – CANADA
PRINTED IN CANADA

CONTENTS

CHAPTER ONE

HOW MUCH DOES MEMORY MATTER?

How important is it to have a good memory? Does it really matter if you have a bad one?

The best way to appreciate the importance of a good memory is to be on the receiving end of a bad one.

Take, for example, this situation.

You arrange to meet a friend for lunch on Wednesday. You struggle through the lunchtime hustle and bustle to the appointed rendezvous and wait – and wait – and wait. Your friend has forgotten all about your date and has blithely gone round to the pub with a colleague.

What is your reaction? Do you think, as you wait in a chilly breeze and then pant back to the office, 'Ah, well, I know he has a terrible memory for dates. Never mind'? Maybe. But you are far more likely to feel irritation; perhaps verging on rage.

If this situation rings a bell with you because *you* are the one who does the forgetting, read on, for it is possible to improve.

One thing is certain: if yours is always the empty place at a dinner party; if you are the one who might pass his own mother in the street without recognizing her; if you can never remember anyone's name, nor what you are supposed to be doing next, nor where you put things, nor what on earth it was you were asked to buy on the way home, the stock cry of, 'I'm terribly sorry, but you see I really do have an awful memory' will not continue to cut ice for long. People will undoubtedly get bored with having to remind you about things all the time, and you will get bored with being constantly reminded, not to mention the ignominy of forgetting!

Absent-mindedness
A bad memory can only be hampering, at work and in social life, but it is not something anyone need be saddled with for

life. A so-called bad memory usually stems from lack of concentration or interest – being 'vague' or 'absent-minded', perhaps only about one aspect of life. Maybe you can remember everything except names, or where you put your spectacles, and things of that kind. The absent-minded professor type has nothing the matter with his memory. It is just that day-to-day matters and trivia are blocked from entering his memory because he is concentrating on the particular problem he is trying to solve. So he does things mechanically – absent-mindedly – and forgets what he has done.

All the memory techniques that people have devised are really only a way of forcing the mind to concentrate for long enough to adapt the system to what you are trying to remember – using a ludicrous picture made from someone's name coupled with the image of his face, or associating some object, such as your briefcase, with something you want to take to the office the next day, for example. You think about it, it goes in and is stored, ready for retrieval later.

So, to say that you were born with a bad memory or that your mind is on higher things is just not good enough. If you improve your powers of concentration, you will be able to remember things as well as the next person.

Surely, if your memory is not all that it might be you must *want* to improve.

'Why is it so important to have a good memory?' you may ask, not at all convinced that you cannot manage just as well with scraps of paper and knots in your handkerchief and a secretary to jog what you call your memory about the important things.

The Efficiency Angle
Take work first of all. You may not feel that your own bad memory matters much, but look around at the people you work with, from a memory point of view.

Let us suppose that two people in particular spring to mind. One always has facts at his fingertips and can switch from one subject to another with 'instant recall'. He can remember the names of all the members of staff, and also something about them and what their particular capabilities are. He can find information quickly and efficiently, has a good general knowledge of his immediate concerns, and about what is going on outside the office, and can read and assimilate quickly and effectively. He remembers dates, appointments, and where he has met people before.

The other person works in constant chaos. His desk is littered with notes to himself scrawled on scraps of paper. His brow is furrowed, he drums his fingers frantically as he stares in desperation at a pinboard covered with more layers of notes. The phone rings and a name is mentioned. His brow becomes even more corrugated as he struggles to think whether he has ever heard the name before. His diary is buried under a pile of papers and refuses to be dislodged. Beginning to feel the onset of heartburn, he tucks the telephone receiver under his chin while he tries to write the name on the palm of his hand, where several shades of ink denote previously missed appointments and forgotten names. His wife comes on the other line to ask if he has remembered to phone the gas man about the leak in the kitchen. His typist comes in to ask if he has remembered to sign his letters. A colleague comes in to ask what has been done about some project which was due yesterday. He realizes that he has lost all the information and finally finds it under yesterday's cup of tea. He sees in a panic that he has forgotten to do anything about it.

If you were told that one of these two was the managing director of the company, would you be able to guess which?

'What rubbish!' you may exclaim. 'I am perfectly efficient in every way. I just have a little trouble with names now and then. And maybe forgetting the odd chore I wanted to do.' Fair enough – you can concentrate on training your memory in that aspect.

Improving One Aspect
Most of us will fall between the two extremes of the paragon and the muddle-head, and want to hone up one particular thing we are bad at. Whatever that is, it can only improve the powers of the memory as a whole to work on it.

Remembering things without having to scrabble about in the files every five minutes will not only create a more efficient impression to observers, but will make you feel far more relaxed, even if you are considered to be perfectly capable so long as you have an aide-memoire up your sleeve. If you are caught away from your filing cabinet and asked what so-and-

so did about so-and-so, it does not look good if you cannot
even remember who so-and-so is, let alone what he did about
anything.

Reading and Assimilating Paperwork
Can you read and remember at work? Or do you start off all
right and then find that you have read two pages without
taking in a word?

You go back to the beginning and this time force one
paragraph into your brain. Then your mind wanders again,
and again you have to go back. A lot of time can be wasted in
this way.

The person who wants to concentrate fully must be able to
clear his mind of all the 'debris' lurking there and clamouring
for attention – what he has to do tomorrow, problems that are
piling up and nagging at him, the people he has to phone or
write to – and think only of what he is reading and trying to
absorb.

So if you are like this and want to improve your memory
processes in this respect, the first stage is to get your mind in
order. Get rid of the clutter and do not let things you cannot
do anything about at the time intrude. It is not as easy as it
might sound to compartmentalize the mind like this, but it
can be done if you are prepared to make the effort.

Remembering People Socially
Socially, too, it is useful to have a good or at least adequate
memory. Maybe, when you try to introduce people to one
another and forget one of the names, you shrug it off with a
'Sorry, I went blank for a minute there, but you know what
my memory's like'. But does the person you've forgotten think
like that? Or does he think, 'He doesn't even think enough of
me to remember my name'?

Another social gaffe, for it must be called this if you are
considering other people's feelings, is not remembering if or
where you have met someone before. Have you ever been to a
party and espied someone whom you met only two nights ago
in a crowd at your local?

'Hallo,' you say cheerily, 'How nice to see you again.'

You are greeted with a blank, confused stare. You wish you
hadn't spoken.

'Don't you remember?' you plunge on desperately, 'We had a long discussion about so-and-so.'

'Oh yes, of course I remember,' the voice is unconvincing, 'You're – er ...'

Finally you have to help out and fill in the details, when you proceed to have an exactly similar conversation to the one you had enjoyed so much only two nights ago.

Remembering faces can be very difficult, and marrying the name with the face even more so. There is not much point in remembering a string of names if you cannot visualize a single face to go with them. But remembering people. is perfectly possible if you use certain techniques to help you. These are described in later chapters.

Remembering People at Work

Remembering people is in fact probably the most important aspect of a good memory, for it makes a marked difference to your relationships generally, at work as well as socially. It makes employees feel good if the boss can remember, not only their names, but also something about them. Colleagues will feel more friendly towards a person who can remember things they have told him. It is far more interesting to talk to someone who can remember a particular problem or triumph you have told him about, than to someone who forgets straightaway and can only look politely mystified when you give him a second instalment.

It is all part of the process of taking enough interest in other people to concentrate on them, listen to them, and think about what they have said long enough to remember it.

Observation

Observation is the first step in memory improvement for no one can remember things if he does not notice them in the first place. That people's powers of observation are generally rather poor has been illustrated many times in the case of witnesses to a crime. Although the accused may have run right past them in an obviously noticeable way, and they may have looked at him quite hard, rather than merely giving him a quick glance, when they are asked to describe him, people tend to have great difficulty in being specific about even such general points as age, height, colour of hair, clothing and so on. Often witnesses will give totally different descriptions of the same person; others will be able to remember nothing but a vague blur.

Think of some of your acquaintances – people you see often, maybe every day. Could you give accurate descriptions of them: height, colour of hair and eyes, facial features, hands, what they were wearing when you last saw them? It is a fair bet that, when you really start to think about it, you will find that you have never noticed these things. You take them for granted, so nothing registers unless they make a violent change in their appearance. Even then it may not strike you straightaway. Maybe you have been in that situation where a friend dyes her hair bright red or has it cut a completely different way, or someone shaves off his beard, or starts to wear glasses. Although you see there is something different, you can't quite put your finger on what it is!

Think of the town you live in. How accurately could you describe to a stranger the position of the various shops in the High Street? How clearly could you direct him to the station or a street on the outskirts, without a lot of, 'Now, let me see – I think it's first left – or no, wait a minute, I know I've seen it – now, I think – I'm not promising, mind – but I *think* it's second left. Try that and ask again.'

Maybe you will scoff at the simplicity of this task but, having been directed into the middle distance, never to be seen again, when all I wanted was the shop round the corner, I still maintain that people can live in a town all their lives and not really *notice* anything about it outside their immediate concerns.

So improving observation is another important step in memory improvement. If you learn to notice things, you will be surprised what you have been missing.

Remembering Appointments

Apart from people and things, though, there are facts and figures to keep in your head. A bad memory can make a lot of extra work for the person who must refresh his memory about everything, even what day of the week it is. He has a diary – but where did he put it? He has a shopping list – but he left it on the kitchen table. He has notes – but he forgets to look at them. He would like to tell that joke – but what was the punch-line?

It may be argued that there is little point in having a diary if you can remember all your dates (or vice versa) – rather in the vein of having a dog and barking yourself.

Take the person who has a right-arm of a secretary who keeps his diary for him, tells him where he is supposed to be at a given time and points him in the right direction. No doubt he also has a wife, mother, sister, lover, flatmate or someone who keeps an eye on the social side of things, buys presents for him to give people on their birthdays, sees that he is around when people are supposed to be visiting, and on his way when he is supposed to be visiting them.

He is certainly taking the easiest way out – and the laziest. It must be admitted by most people that to have absolutely no idea what you are supposed to be doing next is to be too dependent on someone else. What happens when the indispensable secretary is away ill or on holiday? Suppose the prop-and-stay in the home suddenly decides that enough is enough and takes off to the Bahamas for a few weeks. Our reliant person will have twice as much work picking up the strings and getting himself from A to B at the right time, on the right day, and with the right information to hand as he would have done if he had taken some interest in his appointments and had at least a broad idea of who he was going to see during the next week or so.

The diary would then act as an aide-memoire about specifics rather than a crutch without which he is completely at sea.

The business of diaries may cause some controversy for many people appear to think that it is beneath them to remember anything so trivial as an appointment without several jogs from outsiders. But if you take this view, put yourself in the place of the person you have the appointment with.

Maybe he phones the day before to confirm his visit, or to ask for or give some extra information. If you have not the faintest idea who he is, or even that you are going to see him tomorrow, it must make him feel foolish or aggressive, or both. It is unlikely that he will think, 'He's a busy man and I'm lucky to see him at all'; it is far more likely to be, 'If he can't even be bothered to remember who I am, is it worth my bothering to go and see him?'

Remembering Homework

Perhaps he does not phone, but turns up at the appointed time. You have been reminded by your secretary, or by your morning glance at your diary, that he is coming, but you have forgotten again until the moment he enters the office. So you have to collect your thoughts, rummage around for letters, read them through, all while he is sitting feeling uncomfortable and beginning to worry about the time. You thus get off to a chilly and stilted start, instead of launching straight into discussions as you would have been able to do had you remembered that he was coming and that you had a bit of reading up to do *before* his arrival.

So it is worth cultivating a better memory if this is your style. You may say that you have so many appointments in a day that it is impossible to think about any of them beforehand. In that case, maybe you should consider seeing fewer people so that you have a chance to get some value from those meetings you do have, or devising some system for reading up the day before or first thing in the morning.

The main thing is that to give the impression that you could not care less whether you see a person or not, which is what this approach must do, can only create an atmosphere of annoyance and impatience rather than the relaxed and helpful attitude that would no doubt give better results.

Socially, the same thing applies. It is far better not to come home from work tired and harrassed to find your house full of people looking polite and your wife glaring over a deflated soufflé – or your husband searching desperately for your apron and some eggs.

Equally awkward is the phone call just as you are settling down to a nice quiet evening watching television, to ask whether you are ill or have been delayed as everyone is waiting to start dinner. What can you say? Not much.

Remembering Books, Articles, Films

Are you one of those people who can never remember what a book or a film was about? You thoroughly enjoyed it at the time, yet when someone says, 'Have you read/seen so-and-so? What's it like?' you have to reply, 'I have, but do you know I can't remember. I only saw it last week too. Now, what *was* it about?'

This probably does not matter too much with reading for

pleasure, except that you can waste a lot of time reading the same books again by mistake, without, obviously, gaining a great deal from them. But if you are reading to get to grips with a job, or studying for an exam, or reading to get extra background information for your job or learn a new skill, it is very important to be able to retain in coherent form what you read.

It has been said before, but it is worth saying again. To remember what you read, you have to be interested in it. It is the same principle as remembering people and what they say by taking an interest in them. If you are not interested, you will not even get the facts into your mind, let alone retain them.

But, you may say, I was interested in that novel I read and that film I saw. It is just that I have read so many books and seen so many films that I get confused.

This happens when reading or watching films or television is done merely for relaxation or to fill in time. Although there is interest at the time, it is a washing-over, superficial sort of interest. If a book or a statement or a programme makes a real impact on you, really makes you sit up and think, or applies very closely to your own circumstances, you are far less likely to forget it.

Studying

If you found it hard to learn and remember at school, this is no doubt because you were taught to pass exams rather than to become interested in the subjects. It may be that you now remember little and care less about the historical facts and dates you crammed into your brain the night before your exams, or the French verbs you were made to recite, or the mathematical formulae you tried to force through your resistant skull. But if you had an interest in a subject – if you were an ace at English or had a passion for Geography – doubtless you had no difficulty at all in learning, remembering, retaining, and using this knowledge to develop your interest further.

So, for the person who has to study and retain what he learns, parrot-fashion memorizing is not the answer. He has to force himself to concentrate, and understand everything he reads. It is no good chucking some half-understood fact into the back of his mind – even if he does remember it, what is he

going to do with it? In any case, he is far more likely to half
remember it, or remember it inaccurately, if he has not put it
away in his own words, in the context in which it was meant to
be.

'But I can't remember a thing,' some people are heard to
say, 'I didn't learn anything at school – might just as well
never have been there.' Again, this *is* the interest factor – it is
just their bad luck that for some reason or another they could
not muster any interest in *any* subject. But it is a fair bet that
they have not forgotten every single thing that happened when
they were at school. They can probably remember some of the
names of the people they knew at the time, things people said,
stories and jokes they were told, books they read, and the
things they liked doing. Maybe they cannot remember a single
historical fact after the Battle of Hastings, but they can recall
every detail of a football game they played when they were
twelve, or what happened on their first date.

If they had been as fascinated by the course of British
history as they were by their own concerns at the time, they
would probably be able to remember a lot more about that
too! The memory *will* work for everyone if it is applied
properly, and it is never too late to start.

Oiling a Rusty Memory

This type of remembering – learning and retaining what you
read or study – depends upon interest, concentration and
comprehension rather than memory systems, and this will be
gone into more deeply in a later chapter. It may be hard work
to begin with because a memory that has never been forced
into harness before may be rusty and lazy from disuse. It has
become accustomed to telling you that it does not work and
leaving you to write things down so that it can go back to
sleep. You will have to force it into playing its part. You may
have to force yourself to take an interest in something, force
yourself to concentrate, force yourself to remember. But if you
want to improve your memory, you can do so, however much
the evidence of the past aberrations may tell you otherwise.

If you were the type who always preferred to be out kicking
a ball about rather than studiously staying in with your books
when you were at school, or if you were not encouraged to
foster any interest you may have had, so that it died in
infancy, leaving you with a butterfly type of mind, you will

have a more difficult job ahead of you than the person who had a more scholastic background – not in understanding, necessarily, but in concentrating for long periods. You may do well for a couple of pages, then idly begin to wonder what is on the television, or whether you will go and make a cup of coffee, or just gaze at the pages in a daze, thinking of nothing much. But if this is you, don't give up. Force yourself along until the wheels are oiled again.

The importance of a good memory can now be seen in three main areas: people; day-to-day happenings, at work and socially; and reading and studying.

Facts at Your Fingertips
All the aspects mentioned so far apply to work as well as the rest of life, but there is another very important area in the business field. This is remembering in the broader sense – not the minutiae of day-to-day appointments but, like our paragon mentioned earlier, having 'instant recall' about a project or job, or what the current situation about something is, or what you have to do about something else.

There is nothing more off-putting than having a project explained to you by someone who cannot quite remember the details: 'G happened in 1972 – or was it '73? – no, I think – not to worry, doesn't matter anyway – but I'm pretty sure, now I come to think about it, that it was '73. I might just check that if you can bear with me for a moment.'

Nobody can remember everything; or very few people, at any rate. Indeed, it is not desirable to do so, for our minds would become so cluttered up with trivia that they would not be able to cope with the important things. You need to be able to sift and discard irrelevancies. The average person has an average memory; that is, he will not be a persistently forgetful type nor a walking filing cabinet – but he will, if he is wise, try to have an over-all grasp of every subject he has to deal with so that even if he has to check on some of the details, he does not have to fly into a panic, while he rummages in the depths of his brain every time someone asks him a question.

Taking an Interest
Once again, this stems from being interested in your job; or at least, interested enough to understand what you are doing, and what the people around you are doing. This may sound

obvious, but apparently it is not if one goes by the responses to enquiries at more than a few business houses in this country. You may ring someone up and, in his absence, be put through to his assistant or secretary. You may ask, 'Do you know if Mr X has done so-and-so, or written to so-and-so, as we discussed, yet?' and he or she may reply, 'Yes, he did it yesterday.' But he or she is just as likely, in my experience, to reply, 'I don't know. I type his letters but I can't remember really,' or 'Oh yes, I heard him saying something about that but I can't remember what it was now.' Such a response may be caused by lack of communication but it is just as likely to be due to lack of attention and interest.

Remembering Lists

You may rely on notes to remind you what you have to do during a day, or chores you have to see to at home, or a shopping list to tell you what to buy when you go into the supermarket. This is fine as far as it goes, and most people jot things down in this way.

It is a dangerous system, though, if you rely entirely on your notes and make no effort to remember what it is you are writing down. Notes can get buried under a pile of paperwork so that you forget to look at them, or at worst they can get lost, or thrown away. You may leave your shopping list at home or drop it out of your bag, and if something like this happens, you are left with a complete blank, having to go back to square one to try to recompile your list. Or, far more likely, you will simply forget that you had things to remember, chores to do, groceries to buy, until it is too late.

Memory systems are ideal methods of remembering lists of related or unrelated things such as these. If you are concentrating on what you are doing, the mere act of writing something down should help you to remember it anyway, but the peg, chain and association systems are designed for remembering names, dates, lists, facts, appointments – even stories and jokes.

Remembering Speeches, Anecdotes and Stories

You may sometimes have to make a speech and, quite likely, you will want to work in an anecdote or two, but find that you cannot remember any without writing them down word for word. You may feel that you would like to memorize your speech rather than reading it from a piece of paper, but are afraid that you will 'dry' in midstream. Perhaps you have a method of speaking from headings which remind you of the order in which you wanted to bring up points.

You can memorize these points using a system, so that you can dispense with notes altogether, meaning that you will not lose your place, lose your notes, or feel panic rise up in you as you try to recall what on earth you wanted to say next.

As everyone who has to do it knows, speaking with confidence is half the battle in speechmaking. It is embarrassing for everyone, speaker and audience, if the speaker sounds as though he is on the brink of forgetting during the entire speech. Similarly, no one likes to feel that a speaker could not be bothered to learn his speech so decided to read it.

Using a system to remember the key points of a speech and not worrying too much about getting it completely verbatim so long as he keeps on the rails gives a speaker a feeling of confidence: he relaxes and so does his audience.

So a good memory is important, and no matter what yours is like (and if you are reading this book it presumably leaves something to be desired), you can do a lot to improve it.

CHAPTER TWO

IMPROVING CONCENTRATION AND OBSERVATION

How can you learn to concentrate? First, do you know how good your concentration is? Have you tested it?

It may be that you think you are able to concentrate well, or at least adequately. You read a report at work and you get the gist – 'the general idea'. You can discuss the over-all picture and feel that is good enough. But as your eye skimmed over the report, how much did you miss? If someone were to come in and question you on the minute details, would you discover that you had not even noticed they were included?

If a person is unwell or tired, for instance, his brain feels dull, and although he may not be thinking of anything else – except, maybe, how tired and unwell he is feeling – he is not in a receptive frame of mind. There is very little he can do about this except cure the root cause.

If, on the other hand, he is relaxed and refreshed, interested in what he is doing, he is well on the way to winning the concentration battle.

As we all know, there are distractions of mood, too. Bad news may fill your thoughts to such an extent that you are unable to concentrate on anything else. Very exciting news can have the same effect. Trivial worries may nag away at you until they are resolved. Annoyances and arguments may completely 'put you off your stroke', and absorb your thoughts to a disproportionate degree.

Noise is another big concentration killer. The plane flying overhead; drilling the road; music played at full volume; people shouting at one another, are some of the more obvious distractions. But smaller, less noticeable sounds can also pull the concentration away: a tap dripping; the clonk in the central heating that you are counting the seconds for; the murmur of your neighbour's television set; traffic passing by.

Coping With Distractions

Most of us are too easily distracted, for it is obviously not possible to go and live in perfect silence in order to work more efficiently. There will always be phones ringing, people interrupting, and loud life going on all around. You may have noticed the sort of people who can work on a train – maybe, indeed, you are one yourself. Out of their briefcases come files and books and notes, and they read and write and ponder, completely (or seemingly) oblivious to the hustle and bustle going on around them: the 'excuse me; oh sorry, duck' as someone trips over their feet; the five requests to see their tickets; the bellowing conversation of friends who have been separated by six seats; motherly ladies cooing over small children, who in their turn are grumbling or screaming at being told to 'shut up and sit still' by harassed mothers.

What their work is like under these conditions depends how much they can really shut out the noise around them. They may think they are doing so, but outside influences may intervene more than they realize at the time. If you are one of the people who can work under these conditions, you can judge your concentration facility and see whether it is in fact one hundred per cent effective. If not, it could probably stand some improvement to make those train journeys even more useful.

Maybe you work in an open-plan office. Here the problems are similar. There are phones and typewriters and visitors and people holding long, involved conversations about this and that, and others rushing about with coffee, and people going out to lunch and coming in from lunch and having lunch at their desks, and people flying into tempers, getting into huffs or sharing a joke. In fact, there is never a dull moment, but it can make it difficult if you have a lot of paperwork to get through unless everyone else is in a similar 'work to get through' situation.

People may fool themselves that they are concentrating under these conditions too, and then be amazed at the things they have missed or the errors they have made. But, whether it is their own butterfly thoughts or the external influences that prevent them from concentrating, it is not much use blaming anything else except their own lack of tenacity.

Practising Concentration

You can practise concentrating by using some of these exercises.

Try to make your mind a complete blank. Think of nothing at all and do not let external sounds and interruptions break your concentration. You will probably find that you cannot keep this up for more than a few seconds to start with, but try it each day and you are bound to improve. It is also relaxing for the brain to be out of gear for a while: you cannot possibly relax if worries and irritations are chasing each other around in your mind.

Practise reading without allowing your mind to wander. Really make yourself concentrate on every word and if other thoughts try to force their way in, push them aside. Time yourself and see for how long you can concentrate fully. You should improve every day until you can shut out noises, disturbances and thoughts that are nagging at you, and be able to read and work under any conditions.

Study some object, either on your desk or in the room. Look at every detail, concentrate on nothing but that object and see how long you can do this before other thoughts distract you. As you progress, use this approach to think deeply about some aspect of your work, some article you have read, or a more complex matter of this kind. Think about it from every angle, work out the problems or implications, all the time keeping your mind rigidly on the subject. If the mind starts to wander, stop and do something else. Later, try again.

Picture a scene you know well – the street you live in, or some place you have grown familiar with. Try to think about it in detail. Ask yourself questions and fill in as many details as you can. You will probably be surprised at the gaps in your knowledge, but that is where observation comes in. Nevertheless, just concentrate on keeping your mind on the scene, again without distractions.

These ideas are of course merely ways of bending your powers of concentration to your will, so that you can rule them rather than them ruling you. Once you have started thinking in this way, you will find that your concentration improves quickly. Things will 'sink in' whereas before they did not because you were thinking of something else.

One Thing at a Time

The person who tries to do several jobs simultaneously cannot concentrate on any one properly, so if you are inclined to do this, only allow yourself to tackle one thing at a time. Do not try to solve some problem with one bit of your brain while studying some paperwork with another. If things that are not relevant to what you are doing try to creep up unawares, ruthlessly shut them out. As you can only do one thing at once, slot other things into a timetable so that you know you will deal with them – and then put them out of your mind.

Maybe you are the sort of person who is terrified of not doing something as soon as you think about it in case you forget. So while dictating a letter you will suddenly leap up and hunt for something in the files; while reading, you will remember a hundred and one things you meant to do about the house and start mentally doing them while still, to all intents and purposes anyway, reading your book; you will break off in the middle of a job, saying, 'I've just remembered, I must do this, so I'll come back to that.'

This shows muddled thinking and means that nothing gets done properly. You will lose the thread of the letter you are dictating; you are not reading while you are thinking about the chores you ought to be doing – neither are you doing the chores; you will complete neither job well if you break off in the middle of one to do another, and dart to and fro trying to decide what to do next.

If you do suddenly remember something, you could use one of the systems that will be described later to keep it at the back of your mind. Or, if you must, jot it down on your list of things to do. But as part of the over-all exercise, do not break off what you are doing and snap your concentration straight back as soon as you can.

It is far better, though, to sort out what you have to do, make a plan, and then stick to only one thing at a time with as little interruption as you can organize.

Absent-mindedness

Absent-mindedness, as has already been said, is not the result of a poor memory so much as lack of concentration on day-to-day matters – because we are thinking of something else. We all do this because so many everyday actions are carried out automatically that we do not need to think about them. Thus we put things away in a dream, and then of course cannot remember where we put them. Spectacles are a classic example. Everyone who wears them seems to become separated from them at least once a day.

If you are the sort who spends your holidays wondering whether you turned the gas off or locked the front door or shut the windows, don't worry about it. You are not alone. You probably did all these things automatically, but with your mind absorbed in the other things you had to do, or whatever. Therefore you were not conscious of doing them and they did not enter your memory in the first place.

As part of your concentration exercise, though, try to think about everything you do, trivial though it might be. Be conscious of turning off the oven, switching on the kettle, locking the door, and you will find that there is no doubt in your mind as to whether or not you did them. You will soon realize how much time you are saving not having to hunt for something you put down only a minute ago, or track down the coat you left on the train, or puzzle out whether you actually wrote that letter you meant to write, or just thought you did.

Maybe you have envied the sort of single-minded person who can work hard and play hard without ever seeming to mix the two. If a job needs to be done, he can make himself work on it until four in the morning to see it through. If he goes to a party, he can forget about his work, and then switch on again next morning. Too many people live in overlapping worlds: they spend their working hours worrying about the gaffe they made last night, or thinking about what they have to buy when they go shopping, or what they are going to wear tonight, or whether so-and-so will phone, or whether they will phone so-and-so. Then they spend their social hours worrying about something they should have done at work, or the amount of work they have to get through tomorrow, or whether they are making a success of their work at all.

The person who can learn to be single-minded about what he is doing at the time (to be single-minded about any one thing all the time is quite another matter!) will find that his concentration will enable him to get far more done in far less time and he will enjoy life more into the bargain.

Concentrating on What You Hear

It is sometimes difficult to concentrate when people are

talking. This can be the speaker's fault, of course. Boring content or a monotonous voice do not aid concentration – in fact, it is hard to pay any attention to either. But maybe you have asked someone for directions to a place you are trying to find, and when they have finished telling you, you realize that you have not listened to a word.

The art of listening is really the art of concentration. You have no difficulty in hearing what is said, but does it penetrate? And if not, why not?

The answer is: the same old reason – you are thinking of something else.

When you meet new people at a party or gathering of some kind, what do you do? Do you look at them while you are being introduced, noticing their appearance and focusing your attention on them and nothing else? Or do you give them a cursory glance, meanwhile casting an eye around the room to see who else is there? Do you listen when their names are mentioned, or are you thinking what sort of an impression you are making, or whether there is anyone you ought to talk to, so that you are not paying the slightest attention to what is being said?

The most tricky situation is to enter a room full of people and be introduced to the whole lot in one go. There is no way that you can get all their names when this happens, unless your powers of concentration are phenomenal; or, of course, you have become adept with a memory system. There are too many impressions all at once. When this happens to you, see how many names you do get. It is quite likely that it will be one or two at the most – it may even be none. But when you speak to individuals from among this melée, find out their names again, and this time concentrate on remembering them.

You are likely to be caught off your guard meeting people in a crowd. Perhaps you are talking to someone else, or are generally unprepared when you are introduced, and by the time you have collected your thoughts it is too late and the name has gone. So you have to work at people's names under these conditions and make a special effort to find them out and remember them.

Quick Switch of Attention

Meeting someone on a one-to-one basis is quite different. If someone comes into your office and announces his name, and you don't catch it, this means only that you were not paying attention. If a colleague comes in and starts to explain a problem, or gives you some information, and it washes over you without penetrating your consciousness, you have not mastered the ability to switch your attention to the matter in hand. Maybe you were still thinking about what you were doing when he came in, or maybe you were just miles away. But, whichever it was, when he has gone out of the room you realize that you have not the faintest idea what he was talking about, and that had you been able to switch over to him in time, there are a lot of questions you should have asked him.

If you are wrestling with some work which demands all your concentration, it is not easy to change instantly to some other topic. The main thing is to realize this and give yourself time. You could ask him to come back later, or make sure that you are getting what he is saying by thinking it over, and if there were gaps while you were pulling your concentration into line, ask him to recap. Once you have accepted that he is going to talk, focus only on him and what he is saying. Give him your undivided attention.

This applies to every form of listening, be it social chit-chat, a lecture, a briefing for a job, a discussion. The longer a person talks, the harder it is to keep the attention on what he is saying, For instance, it is less easy to stop the mind from wandering during a speech, sermon or lecture than it is during a conversation. Whatever the situation, if you think that your listening ability is not as good as it might be, you should practise focusing on the person who is talking, blotting out extraneous noise and distractions, and giving all your attention to what he is saying. Don't concentrate so hard on concentrating that you don't listen to a word! Later, try to think what was said.

You can test your listening aptitude by concentrating on talks or similar programmes on the radio and seeing how long it is before your mind wanders, no matter how slightly. If it is a subject that interests you, of course, you will have no great problem, but everyone has to listen to talks and discussions on subjects that do not particularly interest him at times, or ones that are put across in a dry and uninspiring way. This is the time when keeping a wandering mind under control will be difficult for someone who has not mastered the technique of focusing on one thing at a time to the exclusion of all else.

Improving Your Observation

Observation is the second main cause of forgetfulness. How can you remember what you don't notice? You can improve your observation in the same way as you improve your concentration – by practice.

You have probably played the party game where you are shown a tray of objects and then asked to write down everything on the tray. People cannot normally remember more than half the things, even though they concentrated on them for half a minute or so.

You can try this sort of thing yourself. Picture a room in your house, or your office – somewhere that you are very familiar with. Try to write a list of everything in that room: furniture, ornaments, pictures, everything you can think of. Now check your list. Go back and look at the room, and note down all the things you have missed. When you write another list, you should do better. It is amazing how much people normally miss without realizing it.

Any situation can be used in the same way. Your route to work, for instance. You travel along it every day, but how much of it do you see? Test yourself by trying to describe it fully, and, next day, start noticing what you have missed, and write another list. Keep this up every day and you will be surprised how much your eyes start to open.

Another trick, described often before, is to try and memorize the articles in a shop window. This is of course the same idea as the tray of objects. Look at the window for a while, noticing the position of the articles and what each costs. Go away and write a list of everything in the window, with the price. Try and visualize the layout of the articles. Then go back and check your list. Try again and see how much more accurate you can be. Keep this up until you can write down every single thing in the window.

Noticing People

The business of noticing or not noticing when someone you know quite well changes his appearance in some way has already been mentioned. Try the same sort of observation tests with people. For instance, visualize a group of people in your office, or some of your friends whom you see often, and imagine that you have to give a full description of them: height, build, colour of hair, colour of eyes, shape of eyes, nose, ears, face, what they were wearing yesterday, hairstyle, whether they wear glasses or have a beard or moustache. You will probably find that you have not the smallest notion about some of these points. As you try to think, the face before you becomes an ever dimmer blur. The next time you see the people, look at them closely and then try the description again. Surprisingly enough, you will probably still forget some things, but here too you will improve as you train yourself.

Try this with strangers, too. Study a face, then try to describe it to yourself. Check on what you missed and try again.

Getting an Impression of People

You may have to make a strong conscious effort to get an impression of someone when meeting for the first time, but if you want to increase your powers of observation and perception and help yourself remember the person later, concentrate on this aspect.

It is not only when there are a lot of people around that difficulties arise. You might be working in your office, absorbed in what you are doing, when a new member of staff is brought in to meet you. You may think that you are looking at him closely and giving all your attention to the pleasantries passing between you, and find later that your mind had not left your work, and you have retained no impression at all.

The best way to keep an impression of someone is to find out something about him on that first meeting. If you confine the conversation to 'how do you do', 'glad to have you with us', 'hope you settle in all right', and generalities of this kind, ten to one the face of the newcomer will be a blur – just another newcomer.

But if you ask him a couple of things about himself – on a general level, not a grilling – such as where he lives, or where he worked before, or anything that makes him an individual in your mind, you are more likely to remember his face when you see it again. The new person will feel happier if a personal approach of this kind is made, too. It is normally perfectly obvious when you are only making a blur of an impression on someone!

When you go to a party, which people do you take to most

when you first meet them: those who talk only about themselves; those who talk only about you; or those who talk a bit about both? No doubt your answer would be the last alternative: the first is boring, the second is grilling, but the third permits a rapport to be established.

For the purpose of getting an instant impression of someone, though, it may be necessary to find out something about him in a very short time. Maybe you can find some small theme that makes a conversation rather than a barrage on your part. And, while he is talking, watch his facial expressions, his gestures, his way of talking. Notice his appearance, his features, his clothes – anything that will fix him in your mind. It goes without saying that no one likes to be scrutinized, so this has to be handled casually, with an expression of interest at what is being said rather than a piercing stare.

Remembering his name is quite another matter, and methods for this will be described in Chapter 4. However, at this stage we are only concerned with studying the person himself, for there is not much point in remembering his name if you can't recognize him when you meet him out of context.

Keeping the Practice Up

You may feel that because you are never likely to see a particular person again there is little point in bothering to remember him. But you never know. Once your memory has been trained in this way, you will not have to think about it, but will automatically observe people instead of glancing at them. To begin with, you should try the technique with everyone you meet until it becomes force of habit.

You may say that you have not the time to waste on this sort of thing; that you meet too many people to take them all in. But it is, after all, a common courtesy to give people your attention when they are talking to you, and that is all you are doing by adopting this method. On the basis that no one can really do more than one thing at a time, it is really no more effort to concentrate on the person you are talking to than to try and fiddle with half-a-dozen bits of paper, or gaze ruminatively into space, working out some knotty problem. Unimportant though the person you are talking to may seem at the moment, you don't know whether he will turn out to be a leading light, or somebody you are going to bump into again two days later. And just think how you feel when people don't remember *you* after a couple of days!

So concentration and observation are the fundamentals of memory training, and if you can improve these powers – and it only takes a bit of effort to do so – it will make you more receptive to the memory techniques themselves.

CHAPTER THREE

READING, STUDYING AND LEARNING

So far we have looked at concentration as applied to general everyday matters such as what people are saying, working in a noisy office and so on. The same principles apply to reading and studying; but here, and particularly in the latter case, the aim is to retain a great deal of information in comprehensible form. There may be problems of understanding what is being read, of breaking down dry and indigestible prose into facts that can be remembered, of extracting the germ of what is being said from a lot of padding.

If you are reading a novel at bedtime, and at the end of a chapter turn out the light and go to sleep, you will probably not remember some of the details when you go back to the book the next night, and you may have to flick back to refresh your memory about certain characters or a sequence of events. In this case, it does not really matter. You are reading for relaxation, to unwind your brain before sleep, and you do not necessarily want anything too demanding to think about.

Reading for retention needs a more long-winded approach than this, though. Some people read the newspaper from cover to cover every day and have a good and wide-ranging knowledge of what is going on in the world. Other people read a newspaper from cover to cover every day and have only the haziest memory of the headlines. The details have completely eluded them. Maybe they are satisfied with just a general idea of what is going on, and only read the whole story because they want to get their money's worth out of their newspaper. Maybe, though, they want to know more but cannot force themselves to take anything in after paragraph one.

Interest In What You Read

As with everything else to do with remembering, the interest has to be there. You have to be extremely interested in politics to digest the parliamentary report every day. The nearest many people get is knowing that there is going to be a Budget, or an Election, or a strike, or cuts in public spending — the things that are likely to affect them. But to really take in what you read, interest and thought have to be there so that it gets beyond the eyes and into the memory. For example, try reading a newspaper article and then making a mental précis of it. What were the main points to remember?

If it was an article about a murder or something similar, you will no doubt be able to remember quite a bit: the victim, the weapon, where the body was found, and so on. These are simple snippets of information to retain; they are eye-catching and do not require too much deep thought. A report on a speech in the House of Commons could be another matter.

Skimming
One method of reading to get the 'bones' out of an article (or book), if you do not need to remember too many details, is to skim through it picking out the main points. You can then see whether, when you put these points together, you have a complete story. If not, you may have missed a link and will have to refer back to the article. But thinking the points and their implications through afterwards helps to fix them in the mind.

This may be all you have time for in the way of newspaper reading, but it should leave a sharper impression than stolidly ploughing through every word while working out what you have to do when you get to the office, or why the train was late – or, indeed, whether you locked the front door!

A method of this kind can come in useful at work too. Suppose you have to get the outline contained in a report so that you can discuss it at a meeting. The meeting is in half an hour and you have not time to read the whole thing properly.

Some people faced with this dilemma would get into a panic and stare at page one in a blood-red haze. Others would start to read every word and would go into the meeting with a good knowledge of the build-up to the plan, but none at all of the plan itself. Quite a few would no doubt appreciate the necessity to skim and try to cram in the main points – but without checking back in their own minds to see if they are retaining anything. Until these people are faced with a query at the meeting they will not know whether or not they have the answer. They will probably recall that they did see something about that, now you come to mention it, but what on earth was it?

The person who will come off best in this situation is the one who picks out the main points, turns the whole project over in his mind from various angles, and tries to find the gaps in his knowledge before someone else does.

Recapping and Linking Facts

Assuming that you want to read more thoroughly than this, how can you determine whether or not you are taking in what you read?

A good way, particularly if the text is dry and hard to grasp, is to read a chunk and then go back over it in your mind, asking yourself what you have just read and what it means. You will soon discover whether or not you have been concentrating because, in order to do this, you have not only to take in the words themselves, but also to understand what is said and how it links up with what you already know or have read on the subject.

For instance, if you read in the newspaper that beef is going up, this fact means something to you because you know what beef costs now, you know how many times it has gone up, and you know whether or not you can afford it. The same applies with other news items; if you follow them daily, each new piece of information relates to what you already know, and so you recognize the implications of what is happening. If, on the other hand, you have been out of touch for a while and suddenly pick up a newspaper in which is continued a story you have not read the beginning of, you are not so likely to be able to take it in. It is harder to gather the background information and get the whole picture.

Applying this idea to reading and study, it is necessary to form an over-all picture of the subject in order to understand the finer points, and thus remember them. The obvious example is learning a list of historical dates without fitting them into the jigsaw of the time. What do they mean when isolated and learnt parrot fashion? Very little.

Picking Out Headings

If some reading matter is likely to prove heavy-going and difficult to keep the mind on, it can be useful to skim through

It first to get the general flow, and then to read it more thoroughly for detail. This can be done by picking out chapter headings, sub-headings, points in the introduction or preface, and points that stand out in paragraphs – the first sentence, for example. Then you will at least know roughly where you are being led.

Now comes the forced concentration bit. Interest has to be maintained, the brain has to keep working and storing the information.

Visualization

The person with a vivid imagination normally manages to get the most out of reading because he sees the scene in his mind's eye. Most people, when they read a novel or book involving people, see the scene, of course. Like watching a film, they visualize the characters, the scenery, every situation that arises. This is not so easy when ploughing through paperwork in the office or studying a textbook. How can you visualize statistics?

But, of course, if you think about it, you can form a picture of anything. If you are reading about a new scheme for the distribution of personnel, you can see the people, what they will be doing and where. A report about a business trip may be couched in pedantic official jargon, but images can still be formed.

Testing Yourself

So you visualize what you read, and keep your interest and concentration up, but how do you know whether you are remembering?

You can apply the same technique as with the skimming method, which is to test yourself on what you have read. Ask yourself questions, and if you cannot answer them, go back and recheck the facts in the book.

When studying for an exam or learning the Highway Code, or learning lines for a play, you may have asked someone else to test you. This is an efficient way of finding the blank spots, but you can make testing yourself equally effective, if not more so. You have to determine what you are trying to learn, what you need to know, and then make sure that you know it.

If it is a new business plan you are studying, and will have to discuss, you need to turn it round every possible way and look for snags: 'What would happen in the case of so-and-so?' type questions. Asking yourself definite questions helps you to pick out the relevant points in the text and also to form impressions and opinions instead of a picture that is furry at the edges.

You have forced yourself to concentrate and take an interest. You have gone over what you have read, you have visualized the scene as you read, you have questioned yourself to test your final knowledge, to see whether you have appreciated what the author was driving at, or whether there are loopholes in the scheme.

Summarizing

Maybe you feel this is enough, and takes up too much time anyway. But in order to find out whether you have assimilated the whole picture and understand it, you can write some notes or a précis in your own words.

You need not write it necessarily. You could visualize yourself explaining it to a colleague or friend; giving him the 'bones' of the book or paper, explaining the points it contained and the conclusions and opinions you have formed.

Writing down, though, definitely helps to put the facts into the memory. Some people underline relevant points in books, so that they can refer to them easily; others make notes in the margin. It is useful to make notes as you go along, in your own words. The mere fact of putting something into your own words shows that you have understood it, because you would not be able to do so otherwise.

So, if you can write a summary in your own words, you have understood what you have read and are therefore likely to remember it. If you miss points, you will need to go back and add those to your information. For instance, if you are explaining a plan or the theme of a book to someone else, they, looking at it from a different angle, may ask, 'But what about so-and-so?' or 'What happened to that?' If you cannot answer their questions, you have obviously missed a link and need to go back over it.

Revision and Repetition

The person who is studying for an exam will have to revise the material periodically to be sure of retaining it all, particularly straight after the learning process, but a read through his

notes and summary should be enough to refresh his memory if
the initial groundwork of learning has been done properly.
Any details that have escaped can be looked up in the original
book, and this adds further cement to the structure.

Some people find that if they have learnt a piece by heart – a
part in a play, or a speech, or a poem – they can do a lot of the
work by reading it over and over again. No active or conscious
learning has taken place at this stage, but the sheer repetition
has done a good bit of the job for them. This is particularly
noticeable when learning lines in a play. Although
professional actors normally have to learn their lines before
rehearsals begin, amateurs do not because their progress is
more leisurely and, not being trained to it, they are not
normally required to throw away their scripts and get right
into the part on day one. So they read their lines while
'blocking' their moves and getting the feel of the play.

In this way, they may associate a line they have to say with
a particular move in the early stages, and one reminds them of
the other. The constant repetition of the lines as they walk
through their parts at these early rehearsals helps to fix them
in their minds and greatly reduces the actual slog of learning
by sitting down to it.

The same applies with any learning. Reading through and
repeating cannot fail to help. It is no good learning something
as thoroughly as possible and then, having abandoned it for
three months, hoping to remember every detail or every line
with accuracy. Everyone needs a 'brush-up' now and again –
preferably fairly often in the early days, to really fix it in the
mind, when it is more likely to stick firmly.

Although you may not be learning word for word –
probably are not, in fact – the refresher has the same effect.
After the first learning, force the facts home and keep checking
them during the next few weeks until you are sure they have
really sunk in. You should then have them readily at your
fingertips for some time to come.

Making Notes
It has already been mentioned that lectures, sermons,
speeches, talks, and other situations in which the listener is
invited to take in a large block of information in one go are the
hardest to concentrate on and retain. Here again, the note-
taking system can prove useful because it makes the listener

put ideas into his own words in concise and comprehensible form. It makes him ask, 'Now, what does that mean? Does it make sense to me? If not, why not? Have I missed something? Or is he blinding me with science? Can what he is saying be made simple?' and questions of that kind. Having asked the question, he can then listen for the answer, or try to work it out from what has been said, or try to capture the missed point later, instead of allowing the whole thing to send him to sleep straightaway.

Listening in this way is not an easy method of learning, for if the concentration flags you cannot flick back a couple of pages to find the answer. The moment has been missed. So you have to keep your interest up the whole time and not allow outside thoughts to intervene.

It goes without saying that the thought 'I must concentrate' is just as obtrusive as any other, and equally efficient at killing what you are trying to take in. It is interest, not the will to concentrate, that has to come to the forefront – getting the mind around the subject and allowing it to absorb the facts, make sense of them, draw conclusions from them, and store them.

CHAPTER FOUR

REMEMBERING NAMES

'I remember your name perfectly,' the Reverend Spooner was heard to say, 'but I just can't think of your face.'

Translated from a Spoonerism, this is a remark that must be being uttered several million times a day as people struggle to hoist back the name to go with the face they know they have seen somewhere or other.

Remembering names is the most common reason for people wanting to improve their memories, for it is the one case in which notes really will not help. You can write down a person's name, but how is that going to help you when it comes to linking it with his face, even if it does help you to remember the actual name? What use is a list of disembodied names – and anyway, who wants to hang around while you flick through your notes saying 'Don't tell me, I'll get it in a minute' as you hope some kind of a bell will ring by seeing the name written down?

Some people seem to be happy to carry on forgetting names, thinking that they can always get round it somehow, and who cares anyway? The person who normally cares is of course the one whose name has been forgotten.

The importance of remembering names has already been mentioned briefly earlier in the book, but it can afford to be stressed, for the sake of those who still think that doing anything about it is too much like hard work, because people's feelings are at stake.

If you are apt to forget names, imagine yourself in a couple of situations where you are the one whose name has been forgotten.

A Social Scene
You have been invited to a party at which you will not know anyone except your host – and you do not know him very well.

You arrive and ring the doorbell. Your host opens the door. Behind him is a cheerful cacophony of party voices.

The first thing that strikes you is a look of blank astonishment on the face of your host. This is politely masked by a welcoming smile, and you think that maybe you imagined it. After all, it was only yesterday that he invited you and there is obviously a party going on.

So in you go, and your host says, somewhat ruefully for underneath it all he is a polite man, 'How nice that you could come. Look, I know it sounds awful, but your name has gone clean out of my mind.'

You remind him of your name, beginning to feel a bit peeved. For argument's sake, let's say it is Mary Thomas.

'Yes, yes, that's it, of course. Silly of me,' your host laughs at his own stupidity, at the same time hanging up your coat,. pouring himself a drink and checking his hair in the hall mirror.

He takes you in to join the crowd, and makes what seems to him a reasonable effort to get you launched.

'Do you know anyone?'

'No, I'm afraid not.'

'Right. Ah, Colin, this is Molly.' (Alternative 1)

'Right. Ah, this is Colin.' (Alternative 2)

'Right. Ah, Colin, this is – er –. You're not going to believe this, but I've done it again!' (Alternative 3)

'Right. Well, just barge in and make yourself at home.' (Alternative 4)

Whichever alternative is chosen, you are off to a poor start.

A Situation at Work

Now you are at work. You have a fairly responsible job in a smallish firm, and when you first arrived you were introduced to the Managing Director. He chatted pleasantly and made you feel at home, one of the team.

A week later you met him in the town – or rather you saw him, smiled and got a puzzled or startled look in return. Then you met him in the corridor. On his home ground, he at least realized that you worked for the firm but as far as he was concerned it could have been as a tea lady, a director or his own secretary. You began to feel irritated, less keen to work, less interested in the fate of the company. You found it impossible to be part of a team if the man at the head of that team had forgotten your existence.

Today you actually have to go and see the Managing Director. He has to talk to you. He has to make some effort to know who you are.

'Ah, yes, Jean,' he smiles, as you go into his office.

'Mary.'

'Of course, of course, Mary. Funny, you look rather like someone else – confused me for a minute.' An urbane try, but really not good enough. There is someone else in the room.

'John, I don't think you know Jean Thompson.'

'Actually, it's Mary Thomas.'

'Thomas – Thomas, that's it. Mary Thomas, a very important member of our staff.'

If you had forgotten *his* name, he would probably have fired you!

Knowing Names at Work

Everyone has to know the name of the person at the top, or the people who are his superiors. But the people who get the best results are the ones who let it work the other way too. In a company, everyone is important, no matter how lowly his job might seem to those in the rarefied atmosphere of the executive suite, and the superior who says, 'Good morning, Tom' is regarded more favourably than the one who gives a curt nod as he sails by on the crest of his own importance.

Such a simple thing as remembering names can make the difference between a friendly team-feeling from top to bottom and a hotch-potch of people who happen to work under one roof. It forms the basis of an acquaintanceship at any level. It makes an individual *feel* like an individual to be addressed by his name. He can begin to feel he belongs. If he has a problem or something to discuss, he is more likely to think of approaching someone about it if he is a personality with a name rather than one of several unidentified objects.

In larger companies a more impersonal atmosphere is bound to prevail because of sheer numbers, but even so everyone can at least know the names of people in his own department or section, and as many as possible outside it. From top to bottom, the importance of the personal touch cannot be underestimated and apologetic flannelling can never be called a substitute.

If you go to a shop regularly and they know your name –

your newsagent's for example – how do you prefer to be addressed: 'Hello, Mr/Mrs/Miss So-and-so', 'Hello, dear/dearie/duck', or with a blank stare? The answer is obvious, but the difference is marked. Once again, someone has taken the trouble to remember your name and recognizes you to go with it – even though you are only buying a newspaper for a few pennies!

So we have established that it is desirable to remember names. It is of course vital, too, to be able to recall those that are important to your job, for here more than just people's feelings may be at stake. You may insult a valuable client, infuriate a superior, lose a promising contract – all because of your vagueness. It is not easy to seem on the ball when the look of desperation in your eyes gives away the blank spot behind.

Having said all that and accepted it, how is it done?.

Listen to the Name

The first thing is to make sure that you hear the name when you are told it. If you do miss it, it is better to say 'I'm sorry, I didn't catch your name', than to let it disappear and hope to pick it up later. If you are introduced in noisy surroundings it is likely that you will not catch the name, particularly if it is an unusual one, so there is no harm in asking for it to be repeated. Most people will prefer this to having their names remembered wrongly – like the person who misheard my own name, Jacqueline Dineen, and called me Denise for ever more.

Surnames and Christian names can cause confusion too. If someone is called William Thomas, it is important to remember that he is not called Thomas Williams. If you are introduced to someone called Charles Robert Smith, is he Mr C.R. Smith or Mr C. Robert-Smith? Some people do have double-barrelled Christian names as well as double-barrelled surnames, and you might even come across a treble-barrelled surname. The pitfalls are endless.

Get the Spelling Right

So the first rule in memory cudgelling is: have no doubt in your mind what the name is in the first place. If you cannot grasp it when it is said, you can always ask how it is spelt. This will help to get it firmly into your mind.

A name that is pronounced in a way totally different from what the spelling would suggest, or one that has different spellings or refinements, may present a minor problem. Cholmondely is an example we all know but do not often come across. Taylor is a common and easy-to-grasp name, but how about Taillyour, Tailleur and some of the more exotic versions? Smith can be Smyth and you can have Thompson, Tomson or Thomson. Then there are the names 'with an e': Clarke, Browne and Greene, for instance.

Of course, if someone says his name is Clark, Brown or Green you probably would not even think of asking him to spell it, so the 'e' might escape you. With the more unusual name that has this double trick to it, there is no alternative but to realize it and take time to get it straight. If the owner of a name thinks you ought to know that it is spelt Beauchamp, remind him of Mr Beecham.

Use the Name

Once you have the name clearly before you, use it as much as possible – sensibly, of course. It will sound ridiculous to slip it in after every phrase, and the unfortunate bearer of the name will be left in no doubt as to what you are up to. Even if you only say it once or twice, and when you say goodbye, that will help to fix the name and the face in your mind. Most people, when they are talking to a friend, will use the name quite often, 'But, Jim, I don't agree with that', 'What do you think, Joan?' and so on, but tend not to use a stranger's name much, particularly if the introduction has been a formal one and they know the person as Mr So-and-so. Even if you are only talking to one person, meaning that there is no real need to use his name for the purpose of identification, make a conscious effort to include it now and then.

These days, introductions tend to be informal: 'Sue, this is Robin Smith. Sue Jones', and so on. In this situation, the two may straightaway become Robin and Sue and the surnames are forgotten – literally. Some people content themselves with a 'Sue, Robin; Robin, Sue' type introduction and leave it at that. You may know someone for weeks and suddenly realize that you have not the faintest idea what his surname is.

If this happens, the only thing is to ask at the outset if you want to learn and remember the name. Knowing him as 'Robin – do you know, I don't think I've ever heard your surname' is not really good enough for the trained-memory person.

So now you have the name firmly in your mind. In order to make it stay there, you first need to make some picture association of the name itself, and then a picture combining the name and the face.

Making a Picture Association

Some names are easy enough to picture because they already mean something: Brown, White, Taylor, Carpenter, Miller, Gale, Groves, and so on. Others are more difficult and may need breaking down into sections, or changing very slightly to mean something. 'Entwistle', for example, could be broken down into 'end' and 'whistle'. The picture could be of someone falling off the *end* of the pier, blowing a *whistle* for help. The effort of making the picture and the fact that you have thought about the spelling and concentrated on that will remind you that the name is Entwistle, not Endwhistle or even Pierwhistle.

I *have* heard of people getting an association mixed up in this way – for instance, Groves and Woods might conjure up the same picture and you might say that it is pot luck which you choose when you meet the person. But do not forget that you do have a real memory and these systems are just ways of making it work for you. Obviously, you need to have the mental concentration when committing the name to memory to think about it, how it is spelt, how it sounds, and so on. This is what you will then associate with the picture.

This system needs a bit of practice before you can form pictures instantly, but once you have got into the habit it will come very easily.

The main thing is to make the picture as ludicrous as possible. If the person's name is Green, it is no good picturing him in a green sweater. That won't stick in your mind. You need to see him with a bright lime-green face, a shock of emerald-green hair, big bottle-green ears. It is not very effective to see a Taylor sitting cross-legged doing a bit of sewing – he could be darning his socks or warming his knees. If you favour the cross-legged posture, he should be sewing with a huge needle and be hung about with tape measures, and surrounded by bolts of cloth. Or you might see a fussy, darting tailor with a mouthful of pins, tape measures flying out from round his neck like streamers, chopping away with a huge pair of scissors. It does not matter what the picture is so long as it is something that sticks in your mind and jogs your memory.

After a while, as you build up more and more pictures, you will use the same thought to remind you of a word each time, and this will make the process even more automatic.

Try taking some names at random out of the phone book and making pictures of them. Choose, if you can, ones that are not too easy to do – ignore the Cooks, Silvers and Turners and try a few tricky multi-syllable ones, for it is these that are more likely to stump you when you use the system for real. Choose ten names to start with.

Some Examples

My ten are: Singleton, Dimbleby, Carrington, Brackfield, Sutherland, Robson, Thurlow, Passingham, McWilliam, and Hansford.

These are not particularly difficult maybe, but serve to illustrate the method. At this stage we are remembering the names only, and will link them with the people later.

Singleton: what will remind me of that? The picture that comes straight to mind is tons of coal. They have been divided up into pairs ready for delivery, and are happily getting to know one another. Among the chattering, laughing one-ton heaps is a single ton who has no partner and is very unhappy. It need not be coal, of course; any sort of ton weight would do; but this is what came to *my* mind so this is what will make me remember.

Dimbleby is a bit like bumble-bee, so I imagine a dim bumble-bee buzzing round in a dunce's hat. Alternatively, it could be dim-bell-bee, so I see, in the dim light of evening, a large bee in an enormous bluebell that monopolizes the garden.

Carrington is quite an easy one, and here we have a ton again. Someone trying to carry a ton-weight on his back, bowed and struggling under the pressure, his legs splaying and staggering, sweat starting on his brow, as the weight pushes him into the ground.

Brackfield is more difficult. Brack does not mean anything as such. You could use brackish or bracket, but there is a danger of remembering Brackishfield or Bracketfield as this is not a particularly well-known name. I would use bracket – a normal wall bracket of some metal – but someone has eaten half of it. Bracket – brack-eat. This reminds you that the whole bracket is not used. So you have someone standing in the middle of a lush green field eating a bracket.

Sutherland: Southernland. See the expedition to the South Pole, or see the South of England on a map.

Robson depends upon the pronunciation: robson or robeson. For the former, I would see a burglar with a black mask over his eyes, creeping stealthily into the bedroom of a little boy who is standing up in his cot crying, calling for his parents. A small boy in a long robe that he keeps tripping over, holding his mother's hand, is a possible picture for the latter version.

Thurlow suggests lowing cows: two cows grazing, the third lowing, two grazing, the third lowing, and so on in a never-ending line. Thirdlow. To make the picture clearer, I picture a black cow, a brown cow and a Friesian in that order all along the row, and it is always the Friesian that is lowing. Again, my real memory will remind me of the true spelling of the name once it has been jogged by this picture.

Passingham is another easy one. A table of people eating a meal, two people standing up, towering above the others, passing an enormous ham from one to the other.

For *McWilliam* I see William the Conqueror wearing a kilt at the Battle of Hastings.

Hansford could become Handsford, so I see two huge hands helping someone as he wades through a ford in a stream.

You may regard these pictures as ridiculous and be able to think of far better ones yourself. But that does not matter. The point is to choose something that reminds *you* of the name. And, although these pictures take a few words to describe, it only takes a second to see them.

Associating Name and Face

The next step is to associate the picture with the person's face. I will use the same ten names and try to suggest how they might be tied in with the name's owner.

First of all, while learning the person's name and memorizing it, look closely at his face, studying the features or noting one in particular that strikes you as memorable, like a large nose, a bald head, thin lips, beetling brows, curly hair – anything you might be able to work in to your association to make it more memorable.

Alternatively, if the face is fairly nondescript, you can merely associate your picture with its appearance as a whole: for instance, you might see someone called Castle with the top of his head cut into battlements, or King wearing a huge crown lopsidedly over one eye. If you can make a vivid picture of some kind, and see the person's face clearly, it will help you to recognize him. But the features must not be a blur, and this is why picking on one and exaggerating it is often a better method if you can do it. Once again, it is up to you to use whatever strikes you first about a particular individual.

Imagine the single unhappy ton with the face of Mr Singleton. Maybe he has a long nose or a jutting chin and this will be pronounced in the mental picture: tears slide down the side of his nose or drip off his chin. Make sure that you see his face as weight-shaped or a ton of coal, or whatever you have selected.

Maybe Mrs Dimbleby has a large mouth and talks a lot with it. So you see the bee in the dunce's hat flying out of her mouth to escape the spate of words, blocking its ears against the noise like a picture in a children's book. Or you may see her peering at a bluebell through sunglasses, when a bee flies out and stings her fat cheek, or double chin, or domed forehead, or whatever you have selected.

Carrington can be the one carrying the ton-weight, and he could be carrying it on his head so that his face is squashing under it. Again, see any predominant feature in exaggerated form: full lips being pressed outwards, large eyes being squeezed shut, big ears pushed out at right angles to his head.

See Miss Brackfield eating a metal bracket in a large field. A close-up of her face could show her long hair becoming tangled in the metalwork, or large white teeth closing greedily for another bite.

Maybe Mrs Sutherland's head could be covered with snow and ice and little, warmly-clothed figures are fighting their way through to plant a flag in the middle. See the snow sliding down her forehead into her eyes, freezing her nose and so on. If she has thin lips, imagine them frozen together in a firm line so that she is struggling to talk as the expedition climbs up her face to the snowy wastes on her head. Or you could see them pushing each other up her beaky nose.

Mr Robson could be the little boy crying for his parents while the burglar cases his room. Noticeable features might be a beard, moustache, horn-rimmed spectacles, a fleshy face, a square jaw, and any of these accentuated make the picture more ridiculous, as he clutches his teddy-bear to his face. If the name is pronounced robe, see a little boy sitting on his shoulder wearing a robe, and sticking his finger into his piercing eyes, sunken cheeks, or whatever.

The Thurlow face must for me be that of the lowing cow. The first two cows have their heads down grazing, but the third's face is raised in a plaintive moo, with the Thurlow features in position – horns sprouting out of a tight perm, or beetling brows and a wide nose above the mooing mouth. (Not a very flattering image, perhaps, but who's to know what I'm thinking?)

Mr Passingham is the giant clutching the huge ham, about to pass it to someone else. Maybe he balances it on one of his large ears or his determined chin as he leans forward to pass it over the heads of the people at the table.

I would see McWilliam as William the Conqueror in kilt and crown, and Hansford wading through the ford – perhaps with large hands pulling him across by his scrawny neck, or jovial mouth.

Choose the Method That Suits You

These pictures are of course very fanciful but again, though they take a while to describe, they are seen in a flash. You may prefer to use a picture more closely associated with a particular feature of a person's face – like someone hitting his long nose or fighting his way through his moustache, or whatever the name suggests to you. Everyone must choose for himself the pictures which will remind him personally of that face and name. One person's ideas will not necessarily do for another, and the ones suggested here are merely given to explain the method and show how it can be applied

The main purpose, as has already been seen, is to force you to look closely at the person's face and notice the features, listen to his name, and think about it long enough to associate ideas and link it with the face. The advantage of choosing a particular feature is that you are more likely to notice this again – your eyes will pick it out when you see the person. The added concentration required to do all this drives the name into your memory and it comes easily to mind; provided, of course, that you *saw* the picture clearly and vividly before storing it away.

Another way of remembering names, if you can do this, is to associate the new person with someone you already know of the same name, or with a well-known personality. This works well with Christian names too. You may always associate a particular Christian name with a friend of yours who has it, so if you can link him or her with the new person, it should help you to remember.

Christian Names
Christian names are easier, in many ways, than surnames because they are normally more familiar. If someone is called Jim or Jane or Sue or Dave, you will probably not have much difficulty in remembering that, whereas there is a much larger and more varied range of surnames to memorize. However, people do have trouble with Christian names too, and sometimes associations can be made for these – for instance, nursery rhymes can be used for some: Jack and Jill, Simple Simon, Mary with her little lamb, Struwwel Peter, and so on. Then there are such characters as Robin Hood, Henry the Eighth, Guy Fawkes, King Arthur, Richard III, and a cavalcade of historical personages who bring an instant picture to mind. There are well-known people of today: those in the public eye whose faces are familiar enough to use for association purposes. Characters in books offer up a wide range of names, from Hercule Poirot to Winnie the Pooh.

If you want to use this method, there must be a character association of this kind for just about every name you are likely to come across.

You can of course treat Christian names in the same way as surnames if you prefer to, and picture something that sounds like the name, but in many cases these might be rather obscure because Christian names are not necessarily formed from tangible words, whereas surnames often are, or an approximate pictureable word can be found.

Several Christian names are straightforward of course, and mean something in their own right: Rose, Camilla, Joy, Rosemary, Jim, Bill, Bobby, Penny, Mick, Nick, Sue, Olive, and so on. Some are fairly simple to convert, such as Dave, dive; Jean, jeans; Mary, marry; Freda, freed her; Barbara, barbarian; Alan, all in; Keith, kith; Daniel, spaniel; and others like these. If something comes to you quickly for a name, you might find this method easier to visualize – it depends what sort of name you come up against.

Associating a Name With Someone You Know

Associating Christian names or surnames with somebody you know personally may prove tricky, particularly in the latter case, unless you have a very wide range of acquaintances (whose names you can remember!) with a varied selection of names. But it can be a useful quick method if you do come across a suitable match.

You may meet someone called Fred Browning, and think, 'He doesn't look like Joe Browning. How is he different?' You see the face of both men together and associate them in your mind's eye. Or maybe you ask him whether he knows Joe Browning, or is any relation, to make the link. The names for this approach have to be chosen with care, of course, or it could be like meeting someone from Australia and asking him whether he's come across your aunt Bessie who lives in Sydney. Memory fixer or no, it sounds a bit daft to say, 'John Smith – well, fancy that. Any relation to Dave Smith of Solihull?' It's more than a longish shot!

Practice makes perfect with all these tricks, and it may seem a bit laborious at first to link up such mental pictures just to remember a person's name. But once into the habit of it, it is surprisingly speedy to do.

CHAPTER FIVE

USING PEG WORDS

The idea of using peg words as a memory aid has been around for some time. Indeed, it is thought that the concept of associating things in an orderly way and forming mental pictures was first realized by Simonides, a poet of ancient Greece. He was able to identify the mutilated corpses of guests at a banquet after the roof had fallen in on top of them, because he had used his technique to memorize where everyone was sitting.

The initial ideas of Simonides were developed through the ages, and more sophisticated versions were devised, for people have always wanted to remember more accurately. Before books were readily available, and were consequently a rich man's luxury, students had to memorize vast amounts of textual matter, and memory.systems were thus taught in European schools during the twelfth and thirteenth centuries.

The peg system itself was originally the brainchild of Stanislaus Mink von Wennsshein in the seventeenth century, but was modified by Dr Richard Grey in the eighteenth century into a somewhat clumsier version of the 'number equivalents' we know today.

This method can be used in a variety of ways, enabling you to remember lists of objects in the right order, telephone numbers, points in a speech or story, things you have to do – you can adapt it to your needs. Because the things you remember are numerically keyed, you can not only remember them in the right order, but backwards or picking points out at random as well. For instance, if you have memorized ten things you have to do, and suddenly want to know what number 7 is, you do not have to run through the whole list to find out. You can remember number 7 in isolation.

The Method

The peg system is based on mnemonics, or substituting letters for numbers, and the only things that really need to be memorized are the consonant sounds for the numbers 1 to 10. As you will realize, you can then use these basic sounds to make up longer numbers, and further peg words are easily learnt.

With the consonants, words are made up to link with each number. It does not really matter what these are, so long as they remain the same always and are things you can make a picture with; there is no point in choosing something abstract that does not conjure up a visual thought. The words are in turn associated with the things you are trying to remember.

The Ten Consonants

The first step is to memorize the ten consonant sounds until you know them backwards, and there are obvious pointers to help you learn them.

1 is always T (or D). The letter T has *one* downstroke.

2 is always N. A small n has *two* downstrokes.

3 is always M. A small m has *three* downstrokes.

4 is always R. The word 'four' ends in R.

5 is always L. The Roman numeral for 50 is L.

6 is always J (or sh, ch, soft G). The letter J is almost like a 6 the other way round.

7 is always K (or hard C, hard G). Two 7's back to back can form the letter K ($\mathcal{K}$).

8 is always F (or V). A handwritten f is sometimes like a figure 8, with two loops (f 8).

9 is always P (or B). The letter P is like a 9 turned round.

0 is always S or Z. The first letter of zero is Z.

People are often put off using the mnemonic system because of memorizing the peg words. However, so long as you remember the phonetic alphabet for the digits, as given here, you can very easily transpose them into words which are not hard to remember.

When the sounds have been well memorized, you can move on to the actual peg words. The first nine are very easy as they are all one-consonant words.

The vowels and the consonants not listed in the key do not have any relevance and can be used to form words as you choose.

Peg Words

The first ten peg words, then, are:

1. *Tea*. Picture a cup of tea, or tea pouring from a pot into a cup.
2. *Noah*. An ark with the animals going in two by two may be easier to visualize. You can add a benign, bearded Noah looking on.
3. *Moo*. It's our old cow again. See that craning, bellowing mouth.
4. *Ray*. A ray of light, from the sun or a torch.
5. *Lay*. See a hen clucking on an egg.
6. *Jay*. See the bird, with its blue feathers.
7. *Key*. An easy one to picture.
8. *Foe*. Picture a stealthily creeping enemy, or a fight.
9. *Bay*. See a beautiful blue sea lapping on to the shore.
10. *Tease*. This is the first example of using two consonant sounds, t and s or z. See someone poking fun and jeering – perhaps a nasty little schoolgirl with pigtails.

These words are always the same so should be learnt thoroughly at this stage. Practise using them to remember lists of things, but do not worry about going further than ten until you are happy that you can recall these pegs and make them into picture associations without having to ponder for long.

Remembering Ten Objects

The following list, memorizing objects in a room, is the sort of thing you might try, to get the idea:

1. Lamp
2. Vase
3. Ashtray
4. Clock
5. Telephone
6. Armchair
7. Fireplace
8. Desk
9. Newspaper
10. Cushion

The idea is to link up each object with the peg word for its number and to make a picture association. Remember that your picture must be as far-fetched and ludicrous as possible. A cup of tea standing next to a lamp on a table is a very normal sight and so it is not likely to stick in your mind. You must exaggerate and make everything bizarre.

For instance, you might memorize the lamp by seeing a huge cup and saucer perched on top of it, or the lamp floating in a gigantic cup of tea, or someone pouring tea from a teapot all over the lamp.

The vase and Noah's ark: you could see all the animals going in two by two, and then two vases following, rolling jauntily into the ark. Or Noah could have two huge vases of flowers at the entrance to the ark, and some of the animals take a mouthful of his floral decoration as they pass.

The ashtray and moo: someone is flicking ash into a cow's mooing mouth, and the moos get louder with indignation. Or, using size again, you could picture a cow trapped in a huge ashtray with high sides, mooing for help as it tries to get out.

Clock and ray: a fairly straightforward one of a bright ray of light shining on a clock, with everything else in complete darkness, would probably be good enough for this one.

Telephone and lay: a hen laying an egg on top of a telephone. Or a telephone clucking as it lays an egg itself.

Armchair and jay: you might see a large jay relaxing in an armchair, smoking a cigarette, legs crossed and not a care in the world.

Fireplace and key: again, both these are quite likely to be in a room together, so you may find size helpful in forming a picture. For instance, a giant key propped up with the fire-irons, or being thrown on the fire to burn. Maybe you see someone trying to sweep the chimney with a huge key.

Desk and foe: you might see a sadistic snarling person hacking the desk to pieces, or ransacking it, throwing papers everywhere. Or, in a fight, one person might wield the desk above his head before throwing it at the other.

Newspaper and bay: you could picture the beautiful blue bay strewn with newspaper, so that it is completely clogged up: or the cliffs could be lined with newspaper all over, with the sea lapping against the sheets and blotting out the print.

Cushion and tease: the horrible little girl might be being smothered with a cushion, or someone might throw a cushion at her as she sticks her tongue out and jeers. Or two children could be having a fight as they float through the air on a huge cushion, the taunting little girl, pigtails flying, poking fun at the other child.

This gives you an idea of the sort of thing you can do to make ridiculous pictures. Using this system, you can remember any one of the objects in isolation. If someone says, 'What is number 5?', you think of the hen laying an egg and remember the picture you have formed.

Of course, you will not want to stop at ten things, but you can form your own peg words for any other numbers simply by making words with appropriate consonants in the right order. You can also memorize long numbers by transposing them into the relevant letters and then making a word or series of words out of them. I personally prefer the latter system, using only peg words up to 99, but other systems have words up to 1000, and again it is entirely up to you what you do. During this chapter, peg words up to 99 have been suggested, but you can merely use this to grasp the system and then make up your own alternatives if you find that easier.

Peg Words from 11 to 30

11. Toad
12. Tune
13. Tome
14. Tar
15. Tail
16. Dish
17. Dog
18. Dive
19. Tap
20. Nose
21. Nut
22. Nun
23. Gnome (a bit of cheating here, but we are concerned with phonetics)
24. Nero
25. Nile
26. Niche
27. Nag
28. Knife
29. Nib
30. Mouse

Again, you may think it is tricky to learn all these, but it is advisable to stick to the same peg words once you have decided on them. It is not as difficult as it looks if you can remember the consonants easily; for instance, you know that

29 must be n and b, so there is not *that* much choice.

Form clear pictures of these, or your own alternatives. For 'tune', picture whatever you are trying to remember singing or with a tune playing from it. See a huge book for 'tome', someone plunging into water for 'dive', and so on.

So now you can memorize thirty things. It is not likely that you will want to memorize the objects in your room for any useful purpose, so what can you do with the system?

Remembering Errands

You can use it to remember the things you have to do, to save writing them down and then forgetting to look at the list. Suppose this is the list of jobs you have to remember in addition to your day's work:

1. Phone the plumber.
2. Take the car to the garage for a service.
3. Pay a cheque into the bank.
4. Phone a friend to accept an invitation.
5. Put up some shelves in the kitchen.
6. Buy a birthday present for your mother.
7. Call for your dry-cleaning.
8. Have a pair of shoes mended.

You do not necessarily want to do the jobs in this order. Indeed, putting up the shelves is presumably last on the agenda, as the other things are daytime, lunch-hour or straight-after-work chores. So the peg system is ideal for memorizing them.

You now make picture associations, as before. Picture the plumber and the cup of tea (try not to be obvious!), the car and Noah's ark, the bank or cheque and the mooing cow, the friend and the ray of light, the shelves and the egg-laying hen, the birthday present and the jay, the dry-cleaning and the key, and the shoes and the foe.

When these pictures are firmly in your mind you can run through them or recall any one easily. All you have to remember is that you have a list of chores committed to memory! If, for instance, you try to phone your friend and can't get through, you store item 4 away to try again later.

It goes without saying that you can equally well remember the things you have to do at work. Just picture your list for the day.

Shopping List

If you have a list of things to buy on the way home, you can use the system to memorize this too, by associating each item and a peg word. You might feel that this is not such a convincing way as writing them down, but if you make a ludicrous picture of each, they will stay with you. Suppose you have to buy eggs, cheese, lettuce, bread, biscuits, and coffee. A suggested picture list might be: a disgustingly greasy fried egg floating in a cup of tea, or someone putting their cup into the middle of an egg so that it splatters everywhere; Noah and the animals nibbling on a giant hunk of cheese that is as big as the ark; a lettuce being stuffed into the cow's mooing mouth; light shining from windows cut into a loaf of bread; the clucking hen pecking away at a plate of biscuits, or sitting on a huge biscuit; and a jay enjoying a mug of coffee.

These are basic little everyday ideas for using the system to save on endless bits of paper and the agony of remembering where those notes are, but there are also several ways of putting peg words to use in the office.

Speeches, Talks, Discussions

For example, suppose you have to make a speech or give a talk at a meeting and don't want to rely on notes. Depending on peg words for this may sound too abstract to make sense, but it is not if you break your speech down sensibly and pick out key points.

Let us say, as an illustration, that you are outlining a new project which you are proposing. You want to begin by giving the background reasons for change: some people are under-employed at present; available space could be used more effectively; it would make the most use of existing equipment and manpower. Then you will go on to describe the scheme – redistributing personnel, combining talents and skills in a more efficient way, thus saving time and money on wasted labour force. You feel that there would be increased overseas interest and that the changes would be good for morale and productivity.

Normally, you might choose to write the key words on a piece of paper and refer to that, which is obviously a better idea than ploughing through a copious mass of notes, or trusting to luck and either drying up in confusion or leaving out some vital point.

Once you are confident about the peg system, though, you can use it with more aplomb than even the scantest notes. These still need to be referred to, surreptitiously or otherwise, and it can ruin a point finished on a high note to have to link it with the next one with an 'er-' and a glance down into your cupped palm.

You may not instantly see the next point if your list is fairly long, and you can still miss things out if your eye runs over them.

If the whole thing is committed to memory, however, you can move more smoothly from one point to another, recalling the next key word as you are reaching the end of the one before it.

Selecting Key Points

So, how would you break down your proposal into manageable chunks that will ensure you remember everything? The first three points are under-employed personnel, using space effectively, and making use of existing equipment and manpower. You can get these down to four words: 1. Personnel; 2. Space; 3. Equipment; 4. Manpower.

These are items which can be visualized and made into pictures with the peg words. Personnel (imagine them lounging around in their under-employed state) with tea – they have so much time to drink tea that they are awash in it, floating in it, but too bored to care; space with Noah; equipment with moo; manpower (now all active) with ray. Form strong and bizarre pictures.

Now you move to the project itself, and here you want to remember the redistribution of personnel, using talents and skills, and saving time and money. Again, you have four more words to use: 5. Redistribution; 6. Talent; 7. Time; 8. Money.

You may feel that redistribution and talent are not easy to visualize, but you do not necessarily have to use your office situation to remind you if something else will do so more vividly. For redistribution you might see figures being moved by a huge hand, like a chess game, or scurrying about hither and thither. For talent, you might visualize an artist painting a huge canvas, or a composer tearing his hair out or pacing the floor, or an actor declaiming a Shakespearean speech. Use whatever strikes *you* as a colourful image. Time can of course be remembered by seeing a clock.

These key words are then linked with the next four pegs: lay, jay, key, and foe.

The last points you want to make are the advantages of the scheme: increased overseas interest; the changes would be good for morale and productivity. The words would be: 9. Overseas; 10. Morale; 11. Productivity, and you would form pictures of these with the next three peg words, bay, tease and toad.

Having done all this, you have eleven points in your head, in the right order, and all you have to do is run through the peg words – provided, as usual, you have used your imagination to create memorable picture association.

The same technique can be used for any speeches, anecdotes, stories, jokes – anything that does not have to be learnt word for word but can just be memorized under precise and logical headings.

Long Numbers

Before beginning to memorize strings of numbers, it will be useful to think about some more peg words. Again, you can make up your own, but this list of words for 31 to 99 may help or give you ideas for your own words. It will also make it easier to explain the method clearly.

As I have mentioned earlier, when memorizing long numbers, it is possible to link the phonetic sounds into longer words – for example, 630 = ch, m, s = chemise. This can get tricky, even with three-digit numbers, for there is not always an ideal word that is tangible, and the result can therefore be contrived at times. For example, if you wanted to remember the telephone number 2016 1017, you could take the sounds n-z-t-j t-s-t-k and try to make something of that, or use two lots of three-digit numbers as is sometimes suggested; you would thus have 201, 610 and 17 or n-s-t, j-t-s, and t-k (17, of course, has a peg word using alternative consonants, dog). But it is often easier to stick to the ninety-nine peg words and, although there may be a word or two more in the sequence, there is not so much difficulty with finding actual words. In this case you would use 20-16 10-17, nose-dish-tease-dog and make a picture sequence of that.

Peg Words to 99

31. Moat	54. Lair	77. Cake
32. Mane	55. Lolly	78. Cave
33. Mime	56. Leech	79. Cub
34. Moor	57. Leg	80. Vase
35. Mole	58. Loaf	81. Fat
36. Match	59. Lobe	82. Fan
37. Mug	60. Chase	83. Foam
38. Muff	61. Jade	84. Fire
39. Map	62. Gin	85. Foal
40. Rose	.63. Jam	86. Fish
41. Rat	64.. Jar	87. Fag
42. Rain	65. Jewel	88. Fife
43. Rum	66. Chichi	89. Fop
44. Roar	67. Joke	90. Boss
45. Reel	68. Chief	91. Putt
46. Rich	69. Jib	92. Pin
47. Rack	70. Goose	93. Bomb
48. Roof	71. Guide	94. Bar
49. Robe	72. Cane	95. Ball
50. Louse	73. Game	96. Peach
51. Lad	74. Gore	97. Pig
52. Lane	75. Goal	98. Buff
53. Lame	76. Cash	99. Pipe

If you find these words easy to visualize and want to use them rather than making up your own, it is advisable to spend some time learning them so that when you think of the consonant sounds, the peg words come to you quickly. If when you have read on, you decide to go for three-digit peg words too, you will have to write these down for easy reference if you want a permanent list. Failing that, you can play each number off the cuff, hoping that you will be able to think of a suitable word at the time, without getting into the realms of complicated and contrived images. As with everything else to do with memory techniques, it is up to the individual to adapt the system to suit his particular needs and apply his imagination to devising the best and most effective way for him.

Telephone Numbers

You may not feel that you want to memorize telephone numbers, that it is just as easy to look them up, but you can be caught out and waste a lot of time. For example, if you want to phone someone in a different area from that which your phone book covers, and you have not noted the number down, you have to waste time phoning Directory Enquiries to find out. It would be far quicker to have the number in your memory file, ready to bring forward when you want it. It takes longer to rummage through files for a letter, longer to ask around, longer to search for your address book or the old envelope you scribbled it down on, or even to find the name in the phone book, than it does to remember.

Nowadays, phone numbers are usually rather long, since the introduction of STD codes, and you may have as many as nine or ten numbers to commit to memory. But so long as you can quickly make up a picture sequence, in the right order, this is perfectly possible.

Suppose you want to remember 6846 54935. You could say, for the sake of argument, that you do not want to memorize any more than ten peg words so you will use a separate word for every digit, but this is unwieldy and can cause confusion if a digit is repeated. Here, for instance, you would have jay-foe-ray-jay lay-ray-bay-moo-lay. Not only is this a complicated jumble requiring lengths of cine film to make a picture association, but jay and lay are each repeated.

So we have 68-46 54-93-5: chief-rich-lair-bomb-lay. I would see a Red Indian chief digging up his riches in a treasure chest and taking them to his lair. He puts a bomb in the entrance so that no one can come in to steal it and sits surrounded by hens laying golden eggs.

It is very important to think of a sequence like this so that you get the number in the right order. See the chief first, then the riches, then the lair, and so on.

A number of this length is one of the more complicated types, and you may prefer, if you are happy that you can remember where the person lives, to memorize the number only and not the exchange code. But, again, once you have got into the habit, it only takes a few seconds to make a picture, so it is worth using the whole number.

Practise memorizing numbers, looking up the peg words if necessary at this stage. It is worth stressing again that you must let your imagination run riot and make the picture as vivid as possible.

Testing Telephone Numbers

Try these for a start:

(a) 520 7314
(b) 96 4723
(c) 2854 653160
(d) 489 8759
(e) 6 921045
(f) 343 8567

It does not matter if you run the numbers together, so long as the order is right. Where zero crops up at the beginning, make up a suitable word using s or z and the letter for the next digit. So, for these numbers, I would have:

(a) lane-sack linking 0 and 7, game-tar
Someone walking down a lane sees a sack full of game (pheasant and so on). As he takes the birds out, a hand pours hot tar all over him.

(b) peach-rack-gnome
A large peach is placed on a rack and tortured by a gnome.

(c) knife-lair-jewel-moat-chase
You are dodging flailing knives to get into the lair to find the jewels. You grab them and run but are trapped by a moat. You see you are being chased.

(d) roof-buff-goal-bay
You see a roof being buffed up, then placed over huge goal posts set in the sea of the bay.

(e) jib-nut-sore-lay
The jib sail on a yacht, and a huge nut on top of the mast. It falls off on a hen on deck, giving it a sore head and crushing the egg it has laid.

(f) Moor-muff-leech-key
For Moor, I would picture a person rather than desolate land, and see him putting on a large muff, then noticing a leech and hitting it with a giant key.

Some systems favour dreaming up one composite picture, but it is then necessary to use other techniques to make sure the numbers are in the right order. If you make a 'film version', you will think the sequence through in the correct order. Another method of getting the order right is to use peg words but memorize them in a chain of links. This system is explained in Chapter 6.

Adding the Name

Now, of course, you want to remember whose number it is you are remembering. This is not as complicated as it may seem because you only have to remember the name, and not the face to go with it, as when meeting a person. You therefore merely need to add a picture of the name to your number sequence, and you have it.

Suppose that the number 96 4723 belongs to Mr Clarke. You simply put in a Dickensian clerk scribbling with a quill at a high desk as he watches the peach being tortured on the rack by the gnome.

If Mrs Rookham's number is 343 8567, see a rook perched on a ham pecking at the Moor's legs as he puts on his muff. Then, when you think, 'Now, what is Mary Rookham's number?' the rest of the picture will come into view.

Appointments

You can use this method to memorize any numbers, of course, so it is a useful one to master. You can devise a system for remembering appointments which lead on from the earlier list of jobs – link the person you are going to see with numbers for the date and time (but always keep the same order to avoid confusion). For instance, the most useful way might be: person, date, time – Mr Salmon, 24, 1115. Make a picture sequence of salmon, Nero, toad, and tail, such as a salmon leaping out of the river while Nero fiddles on the bank, and a toad springing across and grabbing its tail. You do not have to rely on this if you have a diary to refer to, but, if Mr Salmon phones beforehand, the picture you have made will remind you that you *are* seeing him, and when.

If you were seeing him on the 9th at 4 o'clock, you could use 94 instead of 9 and 4, making one word instead of two to remember. So long as you know what you are doing, this should not be muddling; you know you always include date and time in that order, so 29 alone must be the 2nd at 9 o'clock and not the 29th.

You can memorize your appointments for any one day like this, using the name and the time only, and can adapt it to suit your own needs.

Birthdays and Anniversaries

If you want to remember your husband's, wife's or anyone

else's birthday, your wedding anniversary, or some important date in the future, simply link the name or event with the date: wedding-11-6. The months are obviously numbered 1 to 12, so your wedding anniversary is on the 11th of June. If you have two single digits for date and month, you can link them – 24 for 2nd April – so long as you always keep the order the same.

Historical Dates

To remember historical dates, simply form a picture of the name or event and peg words for the dates. It is up to you whether you need to use the century as well as the year: for example, if you wanted to remember 1432, you could either use 14 and 32, or 32 only if you were confident that you knew *roughly* when it was.

This is the most versatile, and therefore the most important, of the memory systems, so take time to become completely familiar with it, adapt it to suit your needs, and make it work for you.

CHAPTER SIX

USING A CHAIN OF LINKS

The chain of links system is a very easy one to use because you do not even need peg words, so there is nothing to memorize. Its use is more restricted than the peg method, however, because items can only be remembered in sequence. You memorize the actual item without a numbered association to hook it to, although the rule about making exaggerated pictures still holds good.

Say, for example, you wanted to remember six things you had to do during the day. These might be:

1. Go to the dentist.
2. Book your holiday.
3. Buy a new umbrella.
4. Play a game of squash.
5. Meet a friend for a drink.
6. Write some letters.

First, you picture the dentist bearing down on you to fill your teeth. When you have a clear mental picture of him, link it with the second item – the holiday. So you may see the dentist, surrounded by all his paraphernalia of drills and so on, lying on the beach covered with sun-tan oil, or going round the people lying on the beach and persuading them to have their teeth out.

As soon as you have formed a ridiculous picture that you will remember, forget the dentist and link the holiday with the next item – the umbrella. See a holiday beach covered by a huge umbrella as the rain pours down; or a holiday resort filled with umbrellas – people holding them over their heads as they eat their picnics, lie on the beach, and so on.

Now forget the holiday and link the umbrella with a game

of squash. You might visualize yourself holding an opened umbrella over you while you play, or trying to play with an umbrella instead of a racquet. Next, link squash with the friend you are meeting, or a drink if you prefer. There could be an enormous glass of beer in the middle of the squash court, which you have to dodge round, or the friend could be standing in front of you drinking while you are trying to play.

Lastly, link the drink or friend with the letters. Maybe you see two huge letters propping up the bar, enjoying a pint together, or your friend struggling down the street to post some enormous letters – or even driving up to your house on a letter instead of in his car.

Now you have a chain of events – but how do you remember the first thing? Obviously, you have to link this to something to start you off. You will undoubtedly remember that you have memorized a list of jobs to be done, so you could list the thought 'jobs to be done' with the first item, the dentist. See yourself scurrying round trying to get things done while he runs after you brandishing a drill or inviting you to 'rinse, please'.

Recalling the Sequence
The main thing with this system is that you must link the items in the order in which you propose to carry them out, because one follows on from the one before. For example, you will first think of the dentist in the list described, and he will remind you of the holiday – but not any of the other things. So if you want to write your letters first thing in the morning, you will have to put them at the top of the list instead of the bottom – unless you want to run through the whole sequence each time.

People sometimes ask whether the things one remembers become confused with this method. They should not if you memorize a list of jobs for one day, do them and then memorize a list for the second day. The first list will fade into the background. You would anyway have to have an appalling memory to forget whether you had done the chores or not! You would just not be concentrating and so would not get any further with really training your memory.

Apart from not being able to remember one item in isolation, this system can be used in many of the same ways as the peg method, and is simpler in some cases.

Lists

It is an ideal technique for remembering a list, such as a shopping list. Again, you merely associate an item on the list with the next and make a bizarre picture. Suppose you wanted to buy apples, cream, potatoes, and soap. These are not the easiest of items to picture in a memorable setting, so use size and exaggeration as much as possible.

First, link shopping to apples – you are fighting your way through an avalanche of apples into the supermarket. Then you see people bobbing for apples in a large vat of cream, or someone pouring cream from an enormous jug on to apples growing in an orchard. Potatoes are swimming through a sea of cream – see their knobbly shapes with arms doing breast-stroke. Then you are peeling potatoes and they turn out to be bars of soap, or you are washing yourself with a potato in the bath.

To prove how quickly these pictures can be formed, try memorizing the following twenty things, and ask someone to check while you recite the list. Unmemorable, everyday things have been chosen purposely, as these are always the hardest to remember.

coat	picture	plate	door
rug	bicycle	shoe	desk
glass	briefcase	knife	pencil
ashtray	envelope	bookcase	refrigerator
book	radio	cigarette	towel

It is really not too difficult to remember a list of this length, provided you are concentrating fully and making sure that you visualize every picture properly before moving on to the next.

Another way you can form pictures is to substitute the second object for the first. If you want to remember to wash the car and mow the lawn, you see yourself mowing the car, or mowing the lawn with the car instead of the lawn-mower. Once again, use whichever association suits you best and springs to mind first.

Speeches, Presentations, Articles

You can use the chain system for remembering speeches, stories, jokes, presentations, and so on, in a very similar way to using peg words. The only difference is that you will link the actual key points you choose instead of using individual associations in numerical order.

In Chapter 5 a method of remembering the key points in an outline of a new project was described. Suppose that you wanted to remember this same outline by the chain of links method.

The key points are: personnel, space, equipment, manpow'er, redistribution, talent, time, money, overseas, morale, productivity.

First, you link personnel with space and make a picture of that; then you link space with equipment, equipment with manpower and so on. And, of course, you would link personnel with the over-all subject of your outline to remind you of the first point.

The slight disadvantage, perhaps, is that all these points are rather abstract to visualize. When using the peg system, you at least have strong peg words to form pictures with, but here you just have two key words.

I would think of some other way of picturing the more tricky words than the office setting – as I described for talent in Chapter 5. Space, for instance, could present a picture of astronauts on the moon; time is obviously shown by a clock; money, perhaps, by a river of coins clanking on to the floor, or notes flying through the air as someone throws a few thousand pounds over his head. The same old point crops up again – use your imagination to make the system work for you.

With the chain system more than with any other, very good concentration is needed to ram the pictures home. The peg system, once you have mastered the phonetics and have the peg words fairly well in mind, does at least present a starting point – you think of, say, twenty peg words that you know anyway and you are halfway, or more, towards remembering what you associated with them. Old Noah may be working overtime if you remember a list a day, but at least he forms a vivid image of something you do not bump into every day of the week.

Remembering by linking does not give you such a clear-cut starting point. It is not so difficult if you are remembering a list of objects or errands, because the pictures of these are usually easily formed into a memorable association, but if you want to efficiently recall the points in a speech, article, book, story, joke, or whatever, firm application is needed to make convincing links between the items.

How Not to Do It

To illustrate the point, let us look at Mr A, who is applying the method in a way which ensures that he will not remember a thing.

One morning he sees an article in a trade magazine that he feels includes information it would be useful to remember. He decides to try the chain method. He begins to pick out key words, and then the telephone rings. He has a chat and hangs up. Now, where was he? Ah yes – key words. He notes some down and as he is engrossed in this, he sees Mrs B passing by outside the window. 'Funny,' he thinks idly, still busily scribbling, 'I thought she was on holiday this week. No, come to think of it, that was last week.' Now he has twelve key words on paper and as he looks at them, his secretary comes in with some letters. 'Blank and Blank just phoned,' she says, 'They have queried a point in their contract.'

Mr A sorts that out, and breaks off from the article to read his letters. Just as he feared, Anybody and Co. won't agree on terms. Problems, problems! With a sigh, he sets aside the article and key words to go back to later.

Later in the day, he manages to snatch a moment to start linking his key words. It has been a busy day and he is beginning to feel bemused. In fact, he can barely remember why it was he was so keen to memorize the points from the article in the first place. His mind keeps jumping back to the other aspects of his work; he finds it hard to concentrate. People keep coming in or ringing up. Instead of being able to use the system in a flash, it is becoming laborious. Still, he perseveres, and manages to form a link-up which he is confident of remembering.

A few days later he decides to bring some of the points from the article into a discussion in a meeting. What were they? Ah yes – but no. His mind is a total blank. In a fury, he curses the system and wishes he had stuck to notes.

Where Did Mr A Go Wrong?

In the first place, he chose an extremely poor situation in which to memorize the points. Even if he had got the whiphand over his powers of concentration, by practising the kind of single-minded application described earlier in the book, would he choose to learn the material in the middle of Victoria Station_ or Piccadilly Circus? Would he find the atmosphere he wanted for tackling some tricky problem in his own sitting room with the television blaring and the children arguing? Very unlikely. He may *think* his mind is fully on the subject, that he is concentrating on nothing else, but the likelihood of this being the case is remote.

So, although he may have had to learn to work in a hubbub, to keep his mind on the job in hand and not let interruptions distract him, given the choice it is not the ideal setting for memorizing. He would have been wiser to take the article home, or to pick a time when there were not likely to be any interruptions of a troublesome kind.

Even so, Mr A could have remembered more despite the distractions, if he had learnt to concentrate. If his mind had been on what he was doing, he would not have noticed Mrs B passing by, nor would he have allowed other points about his work to interfere with his train of thought. He did not give himself a fair chance. Memory systems are really ways of making the mind concentrate while a picture association is formed, thus helping you to remember automatically. If you are thinking of something else or only half concentrating, it is asking a lot to expect your memory to be much better than it was before. Concentration, imagination and visualization are the key points you need to link if you want to get the most out of your memory and the systems that will help to bolster it.

With speeches, written material and things of this kind, therefore, it is imperative to first break them down sensibly and then to really think about what you are doing. If you are memorizing a speech that you have written yourself, it will not be so difficult because you would presumably have been concentrating when you composed it, so your memory should only need a nudge or two to keep on track. But remembering things you read can be an equally important asset, particularly if you want to apply information to a project you are working on, and the link-up method reinforces the concentration techniques described earlier.

Jokes and Stories

You may wish to use the system to remember jokes and stories – for instance, perhaps you like to work one or two into a speech or after-dinner talk. Yet how often have you heard someone telling a joke and getting it all snarled up? Somehow he manages to start with the punch-line and can only peter out lamely with, 'Now, what was it? Ah – no, that's not it. Sorry, I've forgotten' and retire red of face.

Speakers playing safe, therefore, tend to write jokes down, which usually effectively destroys any sparkle they may have had as they are ponderously read out. It just does not have the spontaneity of the practised raconteur.

To remember jokes and stories, and be sure that the punch-line does not slip through your fingers at the last minute, you can again pick out a couple of key points and the punch-line and link these. This should be enough to remind you of the whole story.

Learning By Heart

Maybe you do not often have to learn things by heart – unless you are an actor, or keen on reciting poetry. If you do have to commit something to memory word for word, though, a chain of links can help you along. It will not be a substitute for the slog of learning, but if at the same time you can form an association it will undoubtedly help you to remember and prevent one line disappearing from view.

The technique is exactly the same as for any other link-up method. For poetry, link the first line with the second, then the second line with the third, the third with the fourth, and so on. You may need to choose a word from the line that conjures up a picture to you, or if the poem has rhyming couplets, you may prefer to link the last words. Once you have memorized a verse, or four to six lines, start again with the next verse or chunk. In order to remember how the verses are arranged, link the over-all impression of the first verse with the impression or meaning of the second; the second verse with the third, and so on.

To get the verses word perfect you will have to repeat them often, but the memory aids should prevent you from jumbling lines and verses, or pausing hesitantly while you try to work out what comes next.

Memorizing prose, for a play or verbatim speech, does not have the advantage of rhythm and scan to keep it bowling along from one line or idea to the next but, provided you have done the groundwork of thorough learning, you can link one idea with the next in the same way as memorizing the key words in a speech.

Telephone Numbers

When memorizing numbers, you may prefer to use a combination of the peg and the chain systems. This means that, although you still use peg words for the numbers, you make a chain of links instead of one continuous picture.

For instance, if you are memorizing the telephone number 8963 4281, you would have the words fop-jam-rain-fat but, whereas using the peg system only you would make a composite picture (maybe of a Regency fop eating jam and getting it all over himself, then ruining his frills and furbelows in the rain as he goes to the house of a fat duchess), you would see four completely separate pictures, to include the person whose number it is.

First, link the person's name with 'fop'. To make sure that it does strike a chord when you think of the person's name, if it is someone you know personally you could use an association combining name and face. Say the person's name was Wheeler. You might imagine someone with Wheeler's face making wheels, dressed in Regency silks and satins and an elegant wig. If the number belongs to your doctor, on the other hand, that is an easy association. A fop with a stethoscope, or something like that, would do it.

Then, as with using the chain of links in other ways, you forget about the owner of the number and link fop with jam, jam with rain, and rain with fat.

The advantage of this method is that there is no chance of mixing up the order of the numbers because you only remember one thing at a time and this leads you to the next.

Addresses

You can adapt the chain method to any sort of number learning, and it is particularly good when a picture would begin to get unwieldy. For instance, you might want to memorize an address, and for this you need to include the name of the person, the name or number of the house, the street, and maybe the town or postal code.

To form a composite peg word picture of all this would be complicated and not necessarily reliable. But to link the individual words mentioned in a chain makes sense.

Suppose you wanted to remember this address:

> Richard Baines
> Cedar Cottage
> 124 Wharfside Lane
> Newtown RG6 4JU

Assuming that you are not confident of remembering his complete name without help, and so want to start from scratch, you would first link Richard and Baines by using one of the methods described earlier. For me, Richard straightaway suggests Richard III, and 'bane' means poison, of course. So I would form a picture of Richard III dying a grim and painful death from drinking a goblet of poisoned wine. This picture probably means nothing to you, and you may be using a 'sounds-like' method for remembering Christian names rather than this association of ideas, but I would be confident that it would remind *me* of the name. Everyone must use his own inspiration to put into operation the first picture that occurs to him at the mention of a word. This has been said before, but it is worth reinforcing because that is the only image that will really stick.

Now you have Baines and Cedar – not a particularly easy association, for you must use the poison idea again if one thing is to lead to another. Perhaps you would see thousands of poisoned darts being fired at a huge spreading cedar tree, until it topples over and dies; or someone trying to coax a cedar tree to drink from a bucket of poison, with the same effect. Cedar and Cottage is quite easy. An enormous cedar tree covering a little thatched cottage which stands in darkness, or a cottage perched on top of a cedar tree.

Now things get a little more tricky. The next link is between Cottage and 124, and here I would be inclined to make a link of 124 first, and then link this with Cottage. 124, using the pegs to 99 only, is tune-ray. So perhaps you see someone playing a ragtime tune on the piano, illuminated by a single ray of light. Hear the tune and see the ray of light, in that order, and then make a link with Cottage. Maybe the light shows a cottage on top of the piano. This does mix up the order, of course, so you have to make your proper memory work a bit. You may prefer to link cottage to tune, and then tune to ray, which is following the link system more exactly. My way, I would think of cottage and would see it on the piano (tune) lit up (ray). I would then link this whole picture to Wharfside. The other way, you would have to link ray to Wharfside. Either works quite well.

The rest is straightforwad: Wharfside to Lane, Lane to Newtown, all easy to visualize – until you come to the postal code, RG6 4JU. The problem is not so much finding words to suit as remembering, or distinguishing between, which are letters and which numbers.

Postal codes are usually constructed to a format – two letters, one number, one number, two letters (though there are exceptions) – so I would make up a word for the letters and use a peg word for the numbers. This one might be 'rag' (it could be 47, but you know you have two letters first, and have a set peg word for 47 anyway), jay, ray, and – now we have a problem because a vowel has been introduced and these do not feature in the system, A word cannot be made without using superfluous letters in this case. I would therefore use a word like 'jump'. I know that it would not be a peg word (too many consonants in the 0-99 method), and if I had to remember JM, I would have chosen a word like 'jam'. So the letters must be JU. If that sounds convoluted and illogical to you, you may think of a better way. So long as you devise a method that works for you, and stick to it, it is easy enough to adapt to the not-so-straightforward situation.

Why Bother?

'But why do it anyway?' you may ask. 'Why bother to remember addresses when I can far more easily jot them down in my address book or look in the files?' True enough, but you may not have your address book on you when you meet someone and want to make a note of his address. So what do you do? Probably scribble it on the back of an old envelope or scrap of paper which you put into your pocket and promptly forget about, or turn out and throw away later. The other thing that catches some of us out is writing down a name and address and then, coming across it weeks later, not being able to remember who, when or what it is all about. The concentration required to memorize the name and address should mean that, when you think, 'Ah, now who was that man I met last week? He could be helpful on this,' the situation will come back to you. If you have also linked his face with his name, the chain can begin.

Maybe you do note his name and address on that old envelope first if you have not reached the stage of making instant picture associations; admittedly, you do not want to be gazing at Mr Baines with a perplexed and pondering expression on your face for ten minutes while you work it all out. But then you can quickly commit it to memory later, thus reinforcing it and enabling you to do away with the note. Notes and address books can become separated from you just when you need them most, but your memory file is always with you.

Even if you do not want to use this technique much, it is helpful to practise it as part of your memory training exercise – and you never know when it may prove useful.

Seating Plans

Remembering lists of names in a given order can be achieved easily with a chain of links. This can come in useful if you want to memorize a seating plan or the people at a conference in the order in which they will speak, for example. Obviously, it would only work for organized occasions like this – it would not be any good for remembering the people attending a function because you could not know the order in which they would arrive.

But for a seating plan, for instance, start at one end of the table and work round, making links between names, and faces if necessary. Although it may sound too much of a chore to start with, it comes quickly with practice.

To test your progress, try using the chain system to remember the following lists.

Telephone Numbers
Bell 639 4520
Johnson 0468 21934
Neil 532 6591
Sands 9 8324
Jones 24 2022
Hamble 5981 30222

Names
Mary Smith
Jack Redman
Sue Berwick

David Tindall
Joan Forrester
Tim Hobson

Addresses
34 Worthing Street, Coventry CT3 5PQ.
Treadwell House, Godston Road, Brighton BN22 3TY.
Flat 3826, Acacia Court, Station Road, EJ2 9TM.
396 Rigglesdale Road, Manchester.

Practise these and names, addresses and numbers from the telephone directory or your address book until you are able to think up links quickly. If you devise your own method (for instance, you may be able to cut down on addresses if you know the town or can dispense with the postal code) and keep using it, provided the concentration and application are there, the technique will quickly become one you can automatically adopt.

CHAPTER SEVEN

USING ASSOCIATION OF IDEAS

A technique that many people use, sometimes without realizing it is a technique, is the one of associating something they want to remember with something they will see in the normal course of events.

For example, suppose you wanted to remember to take a book to the office the following day. Rather than trusting to luck and your memory, you might put it on the hall table so that you would see it as you went out. It is easy enough with a tangible object like this, but if you wanted to remember to do something, a similar method would still apply. If you wanted to remember to go down to the shop for a few things, you might leave a shopping bag on the kitchen table to remind you.

This simple technique of moving something from its proper place and putting it in the line of vision as a memory aid is one which people often devise for themselves without any thought of improving the memory as a whole. It is usually used as a guard against absent-mindedness, but is still helpful for remembering little odds and ends. Again, it is only a matter of forcing the mind to concentrate.

Two Alternatives

Mr G wants to remember to take some files home to go through at leisure. He has not time to sort them out as he is due at a meeting, and his secretary is out of her office, so what does he do to make sure he remembers? Maybe the same old thing of writing a note to himself, and it could be that the act of doing this will be enough to remind him. It is just as likely, though, if his mind is on the meeting he is going to and he is in a rush, that he will forget all about the note which has a very good chance of being buried under paperwork as the day goes on.

Maybe, on the other hand, he makes an association between something he will see when he comes back from the meeting and the files. He does not necessarily have to physically move anything – he could just imagine his desk, chair and the floor all around covered with files, sliding and spilling all over the place. He looks at his desk and chair briefly, but hard, while making this association, and when he comes back into the room these objects should jog his memory. If his desk being covered with files is too normal an event to be memorable, he might see his secretary or a colleague scraping away at his desk with a file, or trying to file the desk away in the filing cabinet, or a giant file in place of his desk.

If he cannot see to the files as soon as he comes back to his office, the association should remind him every now and then until he has done so.

G, being a forgetful sort, wants to make sure that he does not forget to take the files home once he has them, so he makes a similar association between them and his coat or the door to his office – the things he will see as he leaves.

H has a memory which fails him too, but his attitude is, 'I haven't time to bother about things like that. Stare at my desk and make a picture association! Ludicrous! I shall remember to see to it when I come back. I've told myself I shall and I shall.' But does he? His mind is full of other matters when he comes back to his office and the files are far to the back of it. Maybe he has gone so far as to write himself a note, which he now sees. Then someone comes in to discuss a point raised at the meeting, H impatiently pushes the note aside and it is soon covered by the papers the colleague has brought in. So H, his mind by now brimming with others things, completely forgets about the files until he gets home that evening.

Remembering at Home

My desk is always orderly and I never lose notes, may be your reply. Fair enough, if that is the way you work. But what about little things you want to remember when you get home? Notes will not be much use there. Some people leave notes to themselves on the floor and going through their houses is like following a paper trail. This is not only untidy but unreliable – once the draught from an opening door has blown that vital note under the sofa, how long will it be before it is found?

Suppose you wanted to remember to post some letters or a parcel. You might put them in your briefcase, so that they will at least leave the house with you. Or you might put them on a table and hope you will spot them and pick them up as you go out. If you want to be sure, you could make an association with your coat or the front door or the front gate. Then, so that you do not forget to post them, make another association with the postbox or post office.

Quick memory aids of this kind can be used for all sorts of little chores you have to do but don't need to make a full-blooded list of. Instead of the absent-minded thought, 'I must mow the lawn tomorrow', make a picture association to remind you; it doesn't take any longer. Concentrate on it – it is all helping to train your memory.

We are back to concentration again, but it has to be mentioned often because it is at the heart of the problem – or the main factor in solving it. If you have tried out the techniques described earlier in the book, you have probably already improved your facility for concentrating. There are, however, some more ways in which concentration and conscious association can help you to remember useful facts.

Facts About People
The method for remembering people's names and faces is clear, but maybe you want to remember more about a person you meet than this. There may be some useful facts about his business that you would like to include, or some details about where he comes from, or his interests.

First of all, a person may have a title of some kind; he may be a doctor, a knight, a serviceman, or a clergyman. If you think you might have difficulty remembering this, use symbols for each profession and associate these with the name: an obvious one, which has been mentioned, is a stethoscope for a doctor.

Working a few facts about people you meet into your associations has a twofold advantage. First, it means that you know more about them when next you meet and, second, putting this amount of thought into remembering them will make the picture all the more vivid.

Jobs
Maybe you want to remember that Miss Knight works in a

bank, or that Mr Crowe sells insurance, or that Mr Jolly is a painter and decorator.

Having thought of Miss Knight in shining armour with the visor wedged on her big nose, or whatever, you can see her in this outfit handing out money in the bank, or counting the notes with gauntleted fingers.

See Mr Crowe as the bird with the man's face – perhaps having spectacles perched in his beak. He is in your sitting room explaining the pros and cons of a household policy. Visualize him holding out the information and peering through his spectacles as he seeks to impress the advantages of his policy upon you. You might prefer to see something else in connection with insurance – that is up to you, but make it vivid to *you*.

Mr Jolly might be roaring with uncontrollable laughter as he slaps paint on a wall. Again, pick out any particular features of his face to remember, and see him balancing precariously on a ladder which is wobbling under the onslaught of his uproarious mirth. This sort of image would be particularly effective if he is in fact rather quiet and dour by nature. If he really is a jolly type, you will probably not have any trouble remembering his name anyway; it comes into the category of Mr Leake, the roofing contractor!

Interests
The same sort of thing can be done with interests or snippets of information you might want to remember about a person. Perhaps Mr Birdsell is a keen sailor, Miss Farmer enjoys photography and Mrs Carter is very enthusiastic about the car maintenance classes she is going to.

You might see Mr Birdsell selling canaries from his yacht as it lurches back and forth on a choppy sea. Perhaps he is sailing around, shouting about the canaries which are in cages hung all over the boat. Maybe Miss Farmer is trying to plough a field with a giant camera, and Mrs Carter is in overalls stripping down a cart while a horse in the shafts looks over its shoulder in surprise.

Remembering where someone lives is usually best done by associating him with a friend of yours who lives in the same town, if this is possible. Otherwise, you can make a picture association with the town and use that.

In each case, it only means adding one thing to your

original picture. To find out these facts about the people you meet, you obviously have to talk to them and listen to what they say, then sift out what you want to remember. This added concentration not only helps you to listen and hear what is said to you, but also makes you retain the picture of face and name for a longer period in the early stages, so fixing it more firmly.

Snippets of Information

You may want to remember odd facts in connection with your work, or something someone has told you, or some little item you read somewhere. Facts of this kind appear in isolation. Earlier in the book, techniques for improving concentration and retention of reading matter were given and one of the main points was: get the whole picture, and link it with what you already know.

The same applies to isolated facts and bits of information you may hear at odd moments. If someone says to you, 'Did you know that Jim Thomas is leaving?' that immediately brings to mind a sequence of thoughts: you know who Jim Thomas is, what his job is, what his leaving means to the company. You might ask, 'Why is he leaving? When is he leaving? Where is he going?' When these questions have been answered, you have the whole picture, or enough of it to remember it.

The same questions need to be asked of any abstract fact you want to fix in your mind. What does it mean in connection with already known facts? Why is it important? Ask any who, when, where, how questions that apply. This is the work of seconds, or a few minutes at the most, but taking this amount of trouble means that the information is correctly filed away, to be associated with relevant facts as they crop up.

Memorizing Vocabulary

So far we have been memorizing things of which we can form a picture: lists of shopping, errands and jobs to be done in the office; facts that can be broken down into key words and visualized. Where the word was not easily visualized, as with some people's names, we broke it down and adapted it to suit a picture we could easily form.

The only things so far that it has not been possible to

visualize are numbers, but here the problem was solved by introducing peg words.

Memorizing new vocabulary may not, on the face of it, seem so easy. Many of the words will be abstract, intangible, not the sort of thing a picture can be made of. Therefore, if we want to associate it with something else, we come unstuck because we cannot see anything vividly enough for it to stay with us.

The method for remembering new words is in fact the same one of association, with one exception. Instead of using the word itself, we use a substitute word. We convert the word we want to remember into one that sounds like it but represents something we can see and associate.

People sometimes use this sort of method unconsciously – or, at least, they remember words they are not sure of approximately because they sound like something else: 'Now, what was that word he said again? Something like jewel, wasn't it?' The association with 'jewel' has been made because the word sounds like it and a jewel is a familiar word that can be visualized.

To illustrate the method, it is simpler to start with words of one syllable. How could the following be memorized easily?

douche; blithe; strop; sough; rend; raze.

Assuming, for the sake of this explanation, that you have not heard these words before and come across them in a book, when you look them up in a dictionary the meanings will seem clear at the time but they will not necessarily stick in your mind. Besides, you only have one thing to picture; obviously the word and its definition cannot be associated. So you find a word that sounds like the one you are trying to remember, and associate *that* with the definition.

A *douche* is a jet of water, normally used medically as in hydrotherapy, but these days more widely applied; for example, 'She was soaked to the skin by a douche of cold water'.

For douche you might choose 'Dutch' as a word which sounds a bit similar. You would then link Dutch with jet of water – perhaps a girl in a winged cap and clogs being soaked by water from a hose or bucket as she walks through a tulip field.

The point is that you have stared at the word as you thought about a substitute for it. You have a picture firmly in your mind, so when you are searching for a word meaning jet of water, the Dutch scene floats up from your memory files; 'Ah, Dutch – douche'. Provided you have noted the spelling and pronunciation when you looked the word up, the concentration used on devising the memory aid will bring the correct word back.

Blithe means gay, joyous. This one is not too easy. It is usually best to find a word with the same first letter, or couple of letters if possible, but in this case probably the closest we can get is a rhyming word 'scythe'. See a joyous, laughing farmer bounding through a field mowing the grass with a scythe. If you were worried about remembering the beginning of blithe, you could see him cut his hand so that it (bl)eeds, but it should be enough to use scythe on its own. Of course, as the meaning of the word is itself abstract, you have to see someone being joyous and cannot make a direct link between the substitute word and the definition (unless you like the idea of a laughing scythe); you have to involve farmer and field for this image. However, the system would not be very useful if you could only use it to remember easily-visualized definitions, so you have to be ready to adapt as necessary and let the application of your memory proper tell you what are the important parts.

See a small farmer with a giant scythe if you want to be sure of getting your priorities right.

When you come across blithe again, the word scythe should straightaway come to mind, bringing with it the vision of the joyous person wielding it. As usual, the more ridiculous the picture the more it will stick.

To *strop* means to sharpen; for example, to sharpen a razor or cutting implement on a strip of leather. You could use 'strip' of leather as the substitute, but it does not give enough contrast for a picture. 'strap' might be better. See someone trying to sharpen a billhook or knife on a strap and cutting it to pieces. Make sure that the sharpening motion is clearly visualized. Perhaps you would choose to see someone trying to sharpen a pencil with a strap.

Sough is a moaning whistling sound, like the wind in the trees. An obvious word which sounds exactly like this is its homonym, 'sow'. You might visualize a fat sow in a sty with the wind whistling round, or the sow looking round in terror at the eerie, moaning sounds.

Rend means to tear or wrench. You could substitute 'rent' and see someone tearing up a rent book in a fury – or tearing up the rent money before the landlord's eyes. You might prefer 'rind', and the picture of rinds of bacon or cheese being torn viciously into tiny pieces – or tearing each other into pieces.

Raze is to destroy completely; 'to raze to the ground'. 'Race' is a possible alternative, perhaps imagined as horses or runners in a race suddenly falling flat all at the same time. This would completely destroy the race and mean that all the runners were on the ground, which should remind you of the definition.

As always, though, these are only my ideas, and words taken at random with an effort to select ones that are not necessarily easy to convert – these are, after all, the ones you are most likely to want to use the sytem for. It bears repeating that it is up to each individual to devise his own methods for remembering, as far as visualizing and associating are concerned.

Association of ideas are at work all the time. Someone may make a remark that reminds you of something you had to do. A story you tell may remind you of something else you wanted to say. A song or a scene from the past may bring back vivid memories of someone you knew at the time. The smell and atmosphere of a house may remind you of your childhood, or another house you lived in. A photograph taken on holiday years ago may remind you of everything that happened on that holiday.

We are using chains of thought all the time. How often have you heard remarks like, 'Seeing you in that dress reminds me of …', 'The smell of Sunday lunch cooking always makes me think of …', 'The sound of the sea always brings back memories of …'?

We cannot choose what chance things will remind us of something else. Often some tiny incident can bring flooding back things we had wanted to forget.

What reminds us? Sometimes the trigger is perfectly logical and understandable. But sometimes it seems insignificant, yet vivid to us; a tone of voice, an attitude, an expression, a chance remark. It would probably go unnoticed by everyone else, and would mean nothing to them if they did notice, but to us it brings back a memory because of its strong association.

The same applies when we are using associations on purpose. What means a great deal to you will probably mean nothing to me, and vice versa. No matter how silly and insignificant it seems, use the first thought that comes to you. The more contrived and generalized it is, the less likely it is to work.

Words of Several Syllables

When memorizing words of more than one syllable, it is usually necessary to break the word down into individual syllables to get separate words that sound like each part, and then associate the pictures created by these words with the definition of the original word, as with the earlier examples.

For example, say you wanted to remember the word 'scaffolding'. There is not one word that you could substitute, so you would break it down into three syllables: scaff-old-ing. For these you might use scarf-old-ink, and picture a huge scarf that is old, tattered and ragged, and covered with blots of ink. Then you would tie this in with the definition of scaffolding: poles and planks providing platforms for workmen while building. Everyone knows what scaffolding looks like so it is easy to see a picture of it, perhaps with the enormous scarf tied to a pole and blowing all over the workmen, or something of this kind.

In this example words have been chosen which very closely resemble the original but, as we have seen, this is not always possible. It aids the memory if the first letter or two of the substitute word is the same as those in the original – or at least sounds like them: scuff/skiff, strike/stroke, and so on. Here just one vowel has been changed to get the new words and although they do not sound exactly alike, enough of the letters are the same to bring them easily to mind. If possible, it is probably best to change the last letter or letters, as in main/maid, mat/mad, but again you have to look for the best alternative in each case.

If you do have to change the first letter, it will be easier to remember if you try to choose one of its phonetic alternatives, as given for numbers in the peg-word system: f might become v; g might become k or hard c; j might become sh, ch or soft g, and so on.

You might want to remember a word that begins with a vowel, or has a syllable that does when you break it down, and to substitute tangible thoughts for this you will have to add a consonant at the beginning of the syllable in question. For instance, suppose 'envisage' was the word you wanted to remember. It would be enough to break it down into 'en' and 'visage', and if 'h' was used to make 'hen', two visual words would emerge. Similarly, with 'amble' you would have 'am' and 'ble', and these could become 'ham' or 'yam' and 'bell'. If you stick to certain consonants for this function – y, h and w are not used in the number substitutes – you will remember that there is a chance it is a word or syllable beginning with a vowel. You might say that if you wanted to remember 'yawl' and 'awl', you would get the same result, but you have the meaning and real memory to aid you. If you did not know the word 'yawl' you would not be likely to use it as an alternative to visualize.

Suppose you wanted to memorize these six words. How would you do it?

1. Combatant: fighter
2. Nuncupate: declare orally, not in writing
3. Navicular: boat-shaped (navicular bone in hand or foot)
4. Extrapolate: calculate something from known terms
5. Mollusc: soft-bodied creature with shell; i.e. snail, oyster
6. Transom: horizontal bar of wood or stone across top of window or door

Combatant can be broken down into com-bat-ant-. The first word that strikes me for 'com' is 'comb', but as the 'b' is silent 'bat' is still suitable for the second syllable. Here, very easily, we have three tangible things to visualize – comb-bat-ant. The picture might be of a fight between a comb, a bat and an ant.

Nuncupate. The definition of this word is harder to picture. To declare orally (normally referring to wills and so on). The word quickly breaks down into 'nun' and 'cupid', which would be near enough, so somehow a picture must be built up of a nun and Cupid with someone declaring something. Perhaps Cupid is trying to persuade the nun to write on a large scroll, offering her a pen, but she pushes it aside and speaks instead. Because this is a more difficult definition to see, it is even more important that it *is* seen and thought about at this stage.

Navicular breaks down into navi-cular or navi-cul-ar. Strictly speaking, the syllables should be nav-ic-u-lar but this is only making unnecessary problems because 'navi' so obviously becomes 'navy'. I would change 'cular' to 'colour' or 'coloured', but you might prefer to break it down further into, perhaps, 'cult' and 'war'.

'Navy' is easy enough – a sailor is the obvious picture for that. Now 'colour' and 'boat-shaped' have to be worked in, and the picture must be out of context and ridiculous. Sailors are usually in a boat-shaped environment, so there is not much point in seeing a logical picture of life on the ocean wave. I would visualize a sailor wearing a large multi-coloured hat shaped like a boat, or something like that.

Extrapolate. Here too we have a tricky definition to picture. I would use a calculator as the symbol for it. The word itself becomes ex-trap-ol-ate. In this case, the first syllable does not lend itself to having a consonant added, and the word that immediately comes to mind is 'eggs'. 'Trap' can stay as it is. 'Ol' could become 'hole'. 'Ate' could stay as it is, but I would favour changing it to 'weight'. So we have eggs-trap-hole-weight and calculator. Perhaps a trap (dog cart) full of eggs going to market tips up and the eggs fall into a hole. An enormous calculator descends and the weight of it crushes the eggs. Or eggs in a big mousetrap in a hole, pinned in position by a huge weight shaped like a calculator.

Mollusc is at least a straightforward definition – a snail, an oyster, a mussel, a limpet. 'Moll' and 'usc' are the two obvious syllables. You might see Moll Flanders for the first bit, or prefer to change the word to something else. I would use 'mill' and 'husk', and see a mill where husks are being removed from snails, oysters and so on instead of from grain.

Transom is another word with a clear definition. It can be broken down into 'tran' and 'som' and the alternative words I would choose would be 'tram' and 'sun'. Concentration on the fact that I have swopped the last letters of each word would serve to remind me that the word is not 'tramson', but if you think this would be confusing you may prefer to choose something entirely different.

I just see one picture of a tram rumbling into the sun (so I only see a silhouette) and going through a huge open door topped by a very wide horizontal bar of stone.

The best way to become quick and expert at finding substitute words and making convincing pictorial associations is to practise the system and see how well you can remember a day or two later. Pick words from a dictionary and write them down, together with their definitions. If you want to test yourself later, you can write the words on one piece of paper and the definitions on another, with the order jumbled. Go back to the lists some time later – say, the next day – and see whether, when you see the word or the definition, the picture you have made comes back to you.

If you have difficulty, it is probably for one of two reasons. First, that you are not concentrating hard enough and actually *seeing* the picture in your mind's eye (it is not enough to say, 'I will visualize a tram, the sun and a horizontal bar on a door – you have to see that picture quite definitely and look at it like a scene in a film); and second, you are not being imaginative and ludicrous enough, or you are not using the picture that comes to mind first.

Speed at using this method will come quite quickly with practice. And practice is the only thing that will really train the memory. *Make* it work.

CHAPTER EIGHT

ADAPTING THE SYSTEMS AND PUTTING THEM TO USE

The systems which will enable you to remember anything and everything, depending on how you apply them, have now been covered, but one or two variations and additions might come in useful or give you ideas for systems of your own.

The mnemonic peg system, as we have seen, has one aspect which some people consider to be a distinct disadvantage and that is the memorizing of 100 or more key words. As I have explained earlier, I feel that this can be overcome by concentrating on making the letters substituted for the numbers 0-9 second nature and using these to form words of your own choice for the other numbers. The method of only going as far as 99 instead of 1000 as some people do, although it may be considered unwieldy in that a string of key words have to be introduced for long-digit numbers, means that it is relatively simple quickly to think of a peg word when only two consonants are involved. A bit of practice should make the ninety-nine words easy to retain as your application to memory training improves. Above all, thought about the construction rather than parrot-fashion learning is the way for it all to make sense and so stick in your mind.

Rhyming Peg Words

However, if you are not convinced and feel it would be easier to go on forgetting, you might prefer another system of peg words, which is to choose some which rhyme with the number. You have to learn these too, of course, but some people find the rhyme easier to remember – rather like 'one, two, button my shoe' and so on.

An example of how this system is developed shows ten numbers with suggested rhyming words that have tangible associations. Pictures are then formed with these in the same way as the mnemonic method.

1. Sun, ton, won, gun
2. Shoe, glue moo
3. Fee, tea, sea, knee
4. Door, war, bore, law (a judge perhaps)
5. Hive, dive, jive
6. Sticks, licks, kicks, fix, mix
7. Heaven, Devon
8. Gate, pate, bait, date
9. Wine, pine, dine, sign
10. Pen, fen, hen, den

The disadvantage with this idea is that it is not so easy to think up words that rhyme with the numbers after 10, and these would of necessity become rather contrived and not very easy to remember. The next ten, I feel, need quite a bit of brain-racking and the results are not very convincing. But, of course, you may not agree.

11. Leaven
12. Elves, delve
13. Flirting
14. Sorting, halting
15. Sifting, drifting, lifting
16. Picking, mixing, fixing
17. Javelin
18. Hating, waiting
19. Signing, whining
20. Gentry, plenty

You would then select words for 30, 40, 50 and so on, and link these with the words for 1 to 9. The system for using the words is exactly the same as any other memory technique – associating ridiculous pictures with the things you want to remember. You might care to adapt this method into a system of your own if you find the general idea appeals.

Maybe you have read through this book and thought, 'It's all tricks to make you remember. It hasn't improved my basic memory.' If you have not troubled to practise as you went along, you would be quite right – it will not have helped your memory. But if you have thought about the techniques described and put them into use, it undoubtedly will have done so. Tricks they may be – or aids might be a better word – but they are making you concentrate, and that, as we have seen, is what memory is all about.

Test Your Memory

If you feel that you are still happy with notes, knots and blank spots, try testing your memory now, using the systems and techniques. You know what your memory was like before. First, memorize the following lists without using any memory aids. Just look at them and concentrate on them. Remember them in the right order, too.

Famous Names	*Any Old Names*
Napoleon Bonaparte	David Jones
Thomas Hardy	Mary Ballantine
Emily Brontë	Fred Brown
Johann Sebastian Bach	Sarah Vernon
Wolfgang Amadeus Mozart	Joan Turner
William Shakespeare	Laurence Dennis
Jane Austen	Susan Berwick
Harry Houdini	Harry James
John Keats	Polly Marriott
Henry Irving	Christopher Elton
Vincent Van Gogh	Sally Russell
Ellen Terry	Bernard Welldon

How did you get on? It is very likely that you remembered more of the first list than you did of the second. The reason is simple. The first list is of people we have all heard of and so, unconsciously or not, we form picture associations of them: Houdini doing a disappearing act; Henry Irving acting; Van Gogh painting or cutting off his ear; Mozart composing, and so on. Portraits of these people are shown fairly often in books and articles so we can probably visualize their faces too. So, although you may not have the order right, you probably remembered most if not all of these twelve names.

The second list, on the other hand, will no doubt have proved more difficult. Who on earth is Joan Turner anyway? As it stands, the name means nothing and so, no matter how hard you gaze at the list, it does not sink in very effectively because there is nothing to associate.

Now try memorizing the two lists again, this time using the systems described earlier.

Test Your Observation

You can test your observation too, by trying some party-type games such as the one where objects on a tray are memorized in a given time limit. If you have time, you could try using the peg or chain system to remember the items. But if your observation has improved with practice, you should be able to recall a lot more just by *looking* than you would have been able to before.

Test your powers of listening and remembering by asking someone to give you a verbal list of objects, names, dates, or whatever you like. The other person should allow a short pause between each item for you to form the picture association. There is no doubt that you will listen much better when you have to apply yourself in this way. There just is not time for wool-gathering.

You might also ask someone to read a passage or news item out to you and see what you can remember of it afterwards. Here, of course, you will not have time to ponder over associations or you will lose the thread, but see if you can get your imagination going to conjure up instant pictures of names, dates, and so on.

You can test yourself best by practising with lists of various kinds until you are thoroughly proficient, then asking someone else to jot down things for you to memorize. If you have to think up and write down the lists yourself, you are starting to remember while you are doing this and, although that is admittedly what you will be doing if you jot down a shopping list or list of chores that you then commit to memory, it is not the ideal test situation.

Here are a few lists to memorize to start the testing off. You could then ask someone to look at the lists while you recite them back, as a guide to how you are doing.

Book Titles

Maybe you are one of those people who set out for the library with a head full of titles you want to read but, on arrival, find that your mind has gone blank. Try memorizing these book titles, with their authors, using the key word method. Pick an over-all thought brought to you by the title and then use the peg or the chain system to remember the list.

1. *Far From the Madding Crowd* – Thomas Hardy

2. *Barnaby Rudge* – Charles Dickens
3. *Pride and Prejudice* – Jane Austen
4. *Coming Up For Air* – George Orwell
5. *Room at the Top* – John Braine
6. *The Power and the Glory* – Graham Greene
7. *The Bottle Factory Outing* – Beryl Bainbridge
8. *A House in Paris* – Elizabeth Bowen
9. *Barchester Towers* – Anthony Trollope
10. *The Moon and Sixpence* – Somerset Maugham
11. *The Beautiful and the Damned* – F. Scott Fitzgerald
12. *A Town Like Alice* – Nevil Shute
13. *The Go-Between* – L.P. Hartley
14. *Odd Girl Out* – Elizabeth Jane Howard

If these books are too familiar to you for test purposes, make up your own list in the same way.

Every time someone says, 'Have you read so-and-so? It's very good,' you can commit it to memory in this way. If you visit the library quite often, you could associate the library with the first title and have an on-going memory chain between visits. This must be better than trusting to luck and standing in the library with screwed-up forehead for half an hour before deciding that it's no good, it's gone – a situation we must all have found ourselves in at times! It is much more reliable than using odd scraps of paper on which to jot down titles, before putting them into different pockets, bags, wallets, never to be discovered again. Give it a try, and before you go to choose some books, run through your mental list to see if it is still there.

Practice Material
Here are some different types of examples to memorize.

Long-digit Numbers

75563254	48573650
38934058	01289751
9672607543	77668833

Shopping List

Potatoes	Toothpaste
Lettuce	Cheese
Soap	Biscuits
Bananas	Marmalade
Tomatoes	Sugar
Bacon	Flour

Errands

Go to the bank
Take the cat to the vet
Have a haircut
Renew insurance
Buy some stamps
Visit an ageing aunt
Return books to the library
Phone Jim Tylor
Buy a birthday present
Pay the gas bill

Fifty Things

1. Donkey	2. Dog
3. Cherry tree	4. Shed
5. Candlestick	6. Spinach
7. Towel	8. Bricks
9. Van	10. Typewriter
11. Television	12. Pen-holder
13. Cardigan	14. Glass
15. Bookcase	16. Rug
17. Pencil	18. Bull
19. Shop	20. Tractor
21. Lamp post	22. Coffee pot
23. Armchair	24. Paintbrush
25. Tie	26. Wine
27: Skirt	28. Cigarette
29. Pier	30. Theatre
31. Letter	32. Pig

33. Cinema	34. Chicken
35. Lorry	36. Door knob
37. Mouse	38. Radiator
39. Tulip	40. Curtains
41. Desk	42. Beach hut
43. Chisel	44. Carrot
45. Refrigerator	46. Hotel
47. Dandelion	48. Rosebud
49. Sand	50. Fireplace

Vocabulary

 1. Liquescent: becoming liquid
 2. Rapscallion: rogue
 3. Quaternary: having four parts
 4. Poniard: dagger
 5. Myosis: contraction of pupil of eye
 6. Termagant: brawling, shrew-like
 7. Inurbane: discourteous
 8. Fulminate: explode
 9. Juxtapose: place things side by side
10. Enigmatic: puzzling
11. Oscillate: sawing like a pendulum
12. ·Pernicious: destructive, fatal

If you practised as you went along, you should have been able to memorize the lists quickly and with no difficulty. Keep practising the system every day so that you find yourself automatically using them to remember. Whenever you find yourself reaching for a piece of paper to make a note, stop yourself and use your memory training. If you really want to make it work, this is the only way.

Writing Notes First
There are some ways in which you can modify the methods to suit yourself and your needs. Writing things down has been mentioned countless times but it can be helpful if you find it easier to *see* something written down before you memorize; the act of writing does of course start the memory process off, if the mind is concentrating on what is being written. Having noted and learnt, you firmly throw the paper away. Don't keep it – that's cheating and reverting to old habits!

Thinking Ahead
Another association system you can use is to imagine yourself

in the situation you are trying to remember. For example, if you want to remember to go to the bank, see yourself in the bank the next day. If you want to remember to tell a colleague something at the office tomorrow, picture the scene. See yourself in your office, then going to your colleague's office. Visualize a conversation between you. Again, this may sound long-winded but it is only another way of filing away a thought so that it comes up when required and does not fall into a bottomless pit.

In Summary

A book of this kind can only generalize and suggest methods for improving, based on the experience of people who have found them helpful. Now we have come full circle and it is up to everyone who wants to improve his memory to sift, adapt, devise and find a way that suits him.

For example, you may know someone who is an ace at remembering names and faces and, because this is such a common stumbling block in the memory stakes, you may think he has no problems. But how is he on facts, dates, errands? Does he *never* say, 'Oh no, I forgot to do so-and-so'?

Most people have some weakness in their memory, although some may be alert enough about every subject for it not to matter too much. It is amazing, though, how many people have some complaint about one or other aspect of their memory. Some people cannot remember anything, others can remember most things, and between them are the majority of us. You may remember facts and figures, but you can't ever find things when you put them down. I might remember names and appointments but not details. He may recall every detail of the book he just read, but he can't remember who lent it to him. She might know everything about every job everyone in her company does – but the names of the people doing them? That's another matter.

Anyone who wants to improve his memory, even if only one aspect of it, should study the techniques as a whole because, as we have seen, they apply to every form of remembering. He should then adapt and use them to suit his own particular mental blanks because they will force him to do the two things that this whole book is really all about – take an interest and concentrate.

That is all there is to it. If your eyes are not interested in what they see, why should they pass the information back to the brain? 'Oh yes, I did vaguely notice something,' you hear people say. Vaguely – what use is vaguely? Vagueness, absent-mindedness, not listening properly, not noticing enough, are the main causes of forgetfulness.

So the secrets are – *listen*, take an *interest, concentrate, recap* on what you have heard or read, *think* what you have done or have to do. The systems in this book are designed to make it easier to do these things by making intangibles tangible. They are just helping you to make your memory work for you.